The World of
Matisse

TIME LIFE BOOKS ®

TIME-LIFE LIBRARY OF ART

The World of Matisse

1869-1954

by John Russell
and
the Editors of TIME-LIFE BOOKS

TIME-LIFE BOOKS, New York

About the Author

John Russell has been on the editorial staff of the London *Sunday Times* since 1945, with particular responsibility since 1950 for art. A contributor to *Art News* and other American magazines, Mr. Russell is the author of books on Seurat, Braque, Max Ernst, Henry Moore and Ben Nicholson. His interest in travel has found expression in books on Shakespeare's country, Paris and Switzerland. Mr. Russell has served on the juries of a number of international art exhibitions and organized retrospective shows of the works of Modigliani, Rouault and Balthus at London's Tate Gallery. A native of London, where he has always lived, Mr. Russell has recently spent a great deal of time in the United States. In his research for this book he has traveled widely, visiting members of the Matisse family and restudying the great collections in Russia, France and the United States.

The Consulting Editor

H.W. Janson is Professor of Fine Arts at New York University, where he is also Chairman of the Department of Fine Arts at Washington Square College. Among his numerous publications are *History of Art* and *The Sculpture of Donatello*.

On the Slipcase

A detail of Matisse's lush portrait of Princess Elena Galitzine posed as an odalisque reveals the painter's love of rich color and bold decorative patterns. (See pages 114-115 for the entire picture.)

End Papers

Front and Back: In these pen-and-ink drawings Matisse combines several of the themes that preoccupied him during the happy period he spent in Nice between the two World Wars; the room is bright with the southern sun, the pretty model reclines on a sofa, the artist himself appears in the picture, either reflected in a mirror, intent and bespectacled *(front)*, or as a hand guiding a pen on paper *(back)*.

TIME-LIFE BOOKS

EDITOR: Maitland A. Edey
Executive Editor: Jerry Korn
Text Director: Martin Mann
Art Director: Sheldon Cotler
Chief of Research: Beatrice T. Dobie
Picture Editor: Robert G. Mason
Assistant Text Directors: Harold C. Field, Ogden Tanner
Assistant Art Director: Arnold C. Holeywell
Assistant Chief of Research: Martha T. Goolrick

PUBLISHER: Rhett Austell
Associate Publisher: Walter C. Rohrer
Assistant Publisher: Carter Smith
General Manager: Joseph C. Hazen Jr.
Business Manager: John D. McSweeney
Production Manager: Louis Bronzo

Sales Director: Joan D. Manley
Promotion Director: Beatrice K. Tolleris
Managing Director, International: John A. Millington

TIME-LIFE LIBRARY OF ART

SERIES EDITOR: Robert Morton
Associate Editor: Diana Hirsh
Editorial Staff for *The World of Matisse:*
Text Editor: Betsy Frankel
Picture Editor: Kathleen Shortall
Designer: Paul Jensen
Staff Writers: John von Hartz, Paula Norworth, Lucille Schulberg, Tony Chiu
Chief Researcher: Martha T. Goolrick
Researchers: Muriel Clarke, Adrian Condon, Susan Jonas, Ann McLeod, Yvonne Wong
Art Assistant: Mervyn Clay

EDITORIAL PRODUCTION
Color Director: Robert L. Young
Assistant: James J. Cox
Copy Staff: Rosalind Stubenberg, Barbara Hults, Florence Keith
Picture Department: Dolores A. Littles, Barbara S. Simon
Traffic: Arthur A. Goldberger

The following individuals and departments of Time Inc. helped to produce this book: Editorial Production, Robert W. Boyd Jr.; Editorial Reference, Peter Draz; Picture Collection, Doris O'Neil; Photographic Laboratory, George Karas; Time-Life News Service, Richard M. Clurman; Correspondents Maria Vincenza Aloisi, Paul Ress (Paris), Bernard Diederich (Mexico City), Margot Hapgood (London), Marti Haymaker (Beverly Hills), Elisabeth Kraemer (Bonn), Traudl Lessing (Vienna) and Ann Natanson (Rome).

Contents

H. matisse 10/39

6

I

"Born to Simplify Painting"

With only a few perfectly placed lines Matisse drew this self-portrait at Nice when he was 70 years old. Striving always for purity and simplicity in his drawings, Matisse made scores of lines in the air before he would lower his hand to the paper. Making sure the image in his mind could be communicated to his pen or brush, he then finished the work quickly.

Self-Portrait, 1939

At eight o'clock in the evening of December 31, 1869, Henri Matisse was born in his grandparents' house in the town of Le Cateau, which lies on the main road from Arras to Sedan in the cheerless far north of France. Sedan in 1870, and Arras in 1914, are grim names in the annals of war, and although Le Cateau itself has quite a bit of style, with an 18th Century archbishop's palace and king-sized formal gardens, the region around it is turnip country: flat, dark and wet. It is a land that has been fought over again and again since Roman times. Le Cateau has been burned to the ground, sacked, shelled, bombed from the air and stormed by assault. Coal mining and the Industrial Revolution have also done their worst. Altogether it takes character to live in this part of France and not go under.

But character is just what its inhabitants have always had. Champions of the region like to point out that the armies of ancient Rome met their match in a tribe called the Nervii, famous as the best foot-soldiers in France, and that the Nervii had their headquarters in what is now Le Cateau. The Spaniards who ruled the region in the late 16th Century bequeathed a certain fierce obstinacy. Mingled with the blood and sinews of the Nervii, it produced a hardy and resolute people.

So goes the legend at any rate, and certainly nothing could be further from the conventional stage-Frenchman than the thick-set, straight-faced, stubborn, industrious, uncomplaining plainsmen of the north. In business they give nothing away, but they can be relied upon. Matisse's father had the right idea when he gave up his job as a linen merchant in Paris to set up as a druggist and grain merchant in the region. He chose the little town of Bohain-en-Vermandois, a short distance from Le Cateau, where his wife's family, the Gérards, had been tanners and glovemakers for centuries. His business prospered, and though he was never rich, by the time young Henri was within sight of the end of his schooldays, Émile Matisse could afford to think of entering his son in one of the learned professions.

Virtually nothing is known of Matisse's childhood and early youth. Until he was 10, he went to the local school in Bohain. Thereafter he was sent to the *lycée* in Saint-Quentin, a town some way to the southwest, where he studied Latin and Greek. If he had any strong feelings about his father's plans to enter him in one of the professions, they have not been recorded. He had no clear idea of what he wanted to do. No special aptitudes or strongly marked inclinations characterized his sober progress from one school to the next. People told him to do things, and he did them, with nothing more than a persistent boredom and an unfocused anxiety to suggest that he had not found his true bent. At 16, Matisse was a square-built, strong-jawed schoolboy going nowhere in particular at a conservative pace. No one could foresee what a perceptive art teacher later foresaw, that Matisse had been "born to simplify painting," and that he would one day change the whole course of Western art.

Yet that is just what Matisse did, and he did it by understanding the genius of France and putting it to use. He saw that genius in its classical terms: lucidity, perseverance, self-knowledge, adaptability, a special feeling for perfection. Others have seen as much, and as clearly, but always with relation to the past; they know what Frenchmen have done, and they try to do it over again. Matisse, on the contrary, knew that what has once been done supremely well cannot be repeated. Twice over in his own lifetime he renewed the whole field of painting. He did it first in 1905, at the Salon d'Automne, when he showed people what high, controlled energy could bring to the handling of color. And he did it again on his deathbed, half a century later, when he produced the huge cut-and-pasted paper compositions that are among the most beautiful objects in modern art. In neither case did the greatness of the work mark the culmination of something; in both cases it was something to be taken up and used by others.

But Matisse as a boy gave no promise of any of this. In fact, he did not even appear interested in art. Although the museum at Saint-Quentin, where he went to school, had some excellent pastels by the 18th Century artist Quentin de la Tour, Matisse at this stage of his life took no notice of them. Neither does he appear to have been aware at the time of the museum at Lille, which was not far from his home and which contained a famous painting by Goya, as well as others by major Dutch and Flemish masters. The public buildings of Le Cateau had a kind of ordered and measured dignity that may have impressed itself upon him as a desirable quality to seek in other departments of life. Certainly the formal gardens of the archbishop's palace, masterpieces of French horticulture in which nature's wild ways are tamed and brought to order, can be read as a metaphor for the importance of lucidity and forethought in human affairs—whoever baptized them Le Jardin de l'Intelligence must have had this in mind. Just as conceivably, Matisse may have seen them as the triumph of patience, planning and coordination over forces usually allowed to run riot. But all of this is conjecture, based on the artist's later activities; it would seem logical, but there is no proof for any of it.

In the fall of 1887, Émile Matisse sent his son to Paris to study law. He went willingly, read his law books, attended his lectures and a year later passed his examinations with exemplary grades. If he was home-sick, nobody knew it; if Paris astounded him, he never said. He spoke only of occupying his spare time with "mediocre distractions." Yet it is a great thing for any young man to spend his 19th year as a student in Paris, and for a young artist—even a latent one—Paris in 1888 was a great city in a great year in a great century. Georges Seurat, composing his canvases with scientifically juxtaposed dots of color, had just completed his poignant comment on the pleasures of big-city night life, *The Parade (page 44)*. Vincent van Gogh had arrived at Arles, where the revelation of southern light and color were to inspire the sun-drenched paintings that have become everyone's idea of the south. Paul Gauguin had returned from a visit to the island of Martinique to question the whole notion of an art bounded by the European past. And working side by side, at Aix-en-Provence, Paul Cézanne and Pierre-Auguste Renoir were striving to find a way out of the impasse that Impressionism had created for itself by its insistence on recording only the fleeting look of a scene at one particular moment.

In short, in the privacy of a handful of studios, the art of the 20th Century was being hammered out. But of this the general public knew almost nothing. Art of that kind in those days was not a topic of public interest, and there were no newsmen or television cameras to peer over the painter's shoulder. To most people, painting meant the historical set-pieces, fraudulent exoticisms and banal moralities, which were being manufactured by artists whose names are now forgotten. Matisse, who cared for neither good painting nor bad, saw no reason to linger in Paris. Having formally completed his law studies, he went back north and took a job as a clerk in a lawyer's office in Saint-Quentin.

It was dozy, unresponsible work. A lawyer's clerk in Matisse's day did what a Xerox machine does now, and often to the same purpose: he copied out reams of information that went into files, never to be consulted. Since bulk rather than content was the criterion, Matisse took to padding his foolscap pages with copies of the fables of La Fontaine. Clients were delighted with the imposing thickness of their files, and Matisse's employer did not complain. At 20, Matisse was embarked in a small way on a professional career, and his future, though not brilliant, was secure.

He could have trundled on in this fashion for another 50 years if he had not, in 1890, got appendicitis. During his long convalescence from the subsequent operation, his mother tried to amuse him with the gift of a box of paints, a set of brushes and a do-it-yourself handbook on painting. The effect was prodigious. The dullness of everyday life dropped away, and Matisse felt for the first time, in his own words, "free, quiet and alone." Never was there a man who was less of a mystic, but a mystic could hardly have spoken more fervently or in more exalted terms of the change that had come over his life. "It was as if I had been called," Matisse wrote 60 years later. "Henceforth I did not lead my life. It led me." These were powerful words for a man who was customarily measured and moderate in speech and in general pursued a rational and systematic existence.

Henri Matisse was twenty when he sat for this photograph with his mother in 1889. Some years later, Anna Gérard Matisse played a charming, though rather incidental role in her son's discovery that an artist's subconscious influences his work. Matisse was in a post office in Picardy waiting for a phone call. "To pass the time," he recalled, "I picked up a telegraph form and made a pen drawing of a woman's head. I drew without thinking of what I was doing, my pen working on its own, and I was surprised to recognize my mother's face, with all its subtleties."

The immediate product of this experience was a collection of copies of the trumpery chromo-lithographs that serve as models for novice painters. The long-term result was Matisse's decision to study art, an undertaking that meant a long and elaborate education at a time when both the nature and function of painting were in the process of being re-defined. There was still an art Establishment, and it was still immensely powerful—so much so that it was hardly possible for a painter to make a living outside it. But it was also clear that the days of the Establishment were numbered. New kinds of art were coming into being that could not be reconciled with the frockcoats and potted palms of the traditional Salon. In fact, a new Salon, the Société Nationale des Beaux-Arts, was founded to exhibit the work of these new artists the very year of Matisse's "conversion."

History is not always a very good guide to the way people felt about things when they happened. Nothing today could seem more expressive of health and well-being than such great Impressionist paintings as Manet's *Bar at the Folies-Bergère* or Renoir's *Luncheon of the Boating Party* or Monet's *Terrace of Sainte-Adresse*. Simply to look at these paintings makes one think how agreeable life must have been at that time. But, in fact, when they were first exhibited, most people regarded them as immoral daubs—flashy, inept and practically incomprehensible —while those most qualified to judge regarded them, at best, as a repudiation of everything that mattered. To academicians art was a matter of trade secrets, and nature was manipulated according to fixed laws. The Impressionists, on the contrary, staked everything on the actual and previously unrecorded look of things. As the name suggests, they saw the world in terms of instantaneous impressions that were to be set down as truthfully as possible.

In theory this was an ideal antidote to the formulas of the academy, but in practice it left something to be desired. The painter abrogated his right to express an individual opinion. He was required to be absolutely passive toward nature, to become, as Cézanne said of Monet, "only an eye." Other painters, in varying degree, also became dissatisfied with pure Impressionism. By the late 1880s they were in full revolt, bent upon finding a kind of painting that would restore to them their freedom of expression. When Cézanne spoke of turning Impressionism into "something solid and durable, like the art of the museums," he had in mind an art of more intellectual substance. He wanted the painter to be able to dictate to nature instead of sitting quietly by, while nature dictated to him.

The pioneers of this new movement were Georges Seurat, Paul Gauguin and Cézanne himself. Cézanne was preoccupied with space. Unlike the Impressionists, for whom space was something vaporous and impalpable, Cézanne regarded space as something to be cut into, like marble. This helps explain why he loved to paint the stone quarries near his home in Provence: method and subject were one. But regardless of subject, in all his paintings he went all out for firmness and hardness and calculation. Seurat, too, reintroduced calculation into painting. In fact, he went much farther than Cézanne, for he believed in the scientific

Just one year after he had first picked up a paintbrush, Matisse—shown here flanked by two classmates—was accepted at the prestigious Académie Julian. But the Académie's staff, led by the award-winning painter Adolphe William Bouguereau, stressed painting in accepted modes; Matisse, disillusioned, left after a few weeks.

analysis of color as well as of space, and he used mathematical formulas to make quite sure that the final effect of his composition was what he intended it to be.

With Gauguin, the revolt from pure Impressionism took an entirely different direction. Romantic biographers like to stress the away-from-it-all aspects of Gauguin's life—how he gave up his comfortable income, his comfortable home and his exemplary wife and children to go off and live a life of seeming debauchery in the South Seas. In fact, Gauguin was a profoundly serious man who wanted to bring a new set of values to the art of his time. He took what seemed to him the only logical step in that direction: he forsook a society that could be content with debased naturalistic painting.

"Man demeans himself when he *adores* nature," Gauguin once said. "He should make use of her." In pursuit of this goal, he broke with the Old Masters and identified himself with quite other sources of energy and enlightenment. He turned to Peruvian idols, to Romanesque sculpture, to Japanese prints, to ancient Egyptian and Assyrian art. "I have tried," he said on his deathbed, "to vindicate the right to dare *anything.* What I have done myself is only relatively good, but every painter who benefits from the new-found freedom of art will owe me something." He was right: 20th Century art, with its contempt for naturalism, its frequent appeals to primeval instincts and its belief in the emotional force of color, is deeply indebted to Gauguin.

This was how matters stood in 1890 when Henri Matisse set out to become a painter. But if Matisse knew that art was on trial, he was also enough of a lawyer to know that every side of a case should be investigated. He was aware that academic art training had in the past produced good work, and he decided to give it a try. Consequently he began his new career by enrolling in a drawing class in Saint-Quentin. The class met every morning from 6:30 to 7:30 and was intended primarily for young people with regular jobs who wanted to learn to be embroidery and textile designers. The hours were grim, especially in winter, but Matisse was a man of indomitable will. He attended class religiously and began to draw everywhere, all the time. "I'd be grateful," his good-natured employer said, "if you could draw a little less during working hours, and be more accurate when you copy my drafts." He also began to paint, in an awkward but workmanlike style.

This part-time activity did not satisfy Matisse for long. It was repulsive in itself, for it seemed a betrayal of his new-found vocation. Beyond that, it was almost meaningless in relation to the distance he had to go and the problems he had to solve. Early in 1892 he announced to his father that he had decided to devote all his time to becoming a painter. The boy who had been listless and docile was suddenly unveiled as a man of elemental determination. "I knew," Matisse said many years later, "that this was the vital turning point in my life. There was something almost terrifying about my total conviction, and about the impossibility of turning back. I just had to put my head down and go at it like a bull at a gate. People had always been at me to 'Hurry! Hurry! Hurry!' Now I heard those words as if for the first time, carried

These two drawings, done by Matisse in 1891 at the Académie Julian, reflect prevailing art-school philosophy: excellence in making unimaginative copies, from a cast *(top)* or nature. It was requirements such as having to sit through 20 classes on drawing plaster casts that prompted Matisse to leave the school and rebel against the dictum, "*Copiez bêtement la nature*"—Copy nature stupidly (doggedly).

along as I was by a power quite alien to my life as a 'normal' man."

His father's first reaction was, "You'll die of hunger!", and at one stage in Matisse's career this prediction very nearly came true. Nevertheless, Émile Matisse decided in the end to let his son try his luck, and even gave him a modest allowance. In October 1892, Matisse was back in Paris, this time as an art student. His father was encouraged to hear that he was taking lessons from Adolphe Bouguereau, then the most famous painter in France, but Matisse soon had other ideas about his new teacher. Bouguereau's paintings now look both lascivious and picayune, with their agglomerations of female nudes and their soapy, standardized methods of presentation. Matisse was not impressed by them. He was even less impressed by Bouguereau's lordly way of copying himself over and over again before an admiring audience. Matisse did not want to be a copyist; he wanted to get to the bottom of art. Before long he realized that the only place to do so was at the École des Beaux-Arts, France's official, government-supported art school.

In 1892 Matisse began his studies under dapper Gustave Moreau. The above lithograph of Moreau, by Matisse's classmate Georges Rouault, was most likely inspired by the jaunty photograph at top. Moreau's philosophy, which stressed personal vision above mere technical competence, strongly influenced the young Matisse.

The École des Beaux-Arts of the 1890s is nowadays regarded as a citadel of prejudice, garrisoned by boors and drudges, and patrolled at infrequent intervals by bemedaled "masters" for whom posterity has a far less impressive name. Nevertheless, it offered resources far beyond the means of any individual student: studios, a huge library, a famous collection of copies and casts, a chance to compete for worthwhile prizes, and—perhaps most important of all—the company of other gifted young people. Matisse was rejected as insufficiently qualified when he first applied for admission. Subsequently he took to sketching, along with other aspiring artists, in the school's glass-roofed courtyard, which contained copies of Europe's great art treasures—paintings by the Italian masters, casts of Renaissance and Greek and Roman sculpture. Most of the "masters" who passed through the courtyard on the way to their classes took a lofty and sardonic attitude toward the would-be students. But there was one exception, Gustave Moreau, who, at 66, had just joined the Beaux-Arts faculty. At first sight of Matisse's drawings, Moreau issued a fateful invitation. "Join my class if you want to," he said, "and I'll fix it up later with the administration."

Today, after more than half a century of exposure to theories of psychoanalysis, anyone would recognize Gustave Moreau as the very type of the sublimated homosexual. A shy, delicate, mother-bound bachelor, with a private income, he led an almost hermetic life in the house on the Rue de la Rochefoucauld that is now the Musée Gustave Moreau. Cutting himself off from the outside world, Moreau lived almost entirely among the products of his own luxuriant imagination. He worked constantly and, at his death in 1898, left the French nation 609 oils, 282 watercolors and over 7,000 drawings.

Moreau in his art was indifferent to the modern world, and chose instead to portray a world of pure fantasy. His paintings are peopled with figures from antiquity—Hercules, Salome, Orestes, Jupiter—in the guise of elegant apparitions, indeterminate in sex and equivocal in their states of undress. Poets and "decadent" novelists like J.K. Huysmans took particular delight in Moreau's sumptuous imaginings. Others, however, thought there was something humbug about his rejection of the normal world. "Moreau," said his old friend Edgar Degas, "is a hermit who knows all the railroad schedules."

In 1892 Moreau turned to teaching. The tender attention he lavished on his students may well have been an outlet for the homosexuality he dared not express. But his classes at the Beaux-Arts quickly became famous for the enthusiasm he aroused in his students and the variety of talents he uncovered. Moreau was the first of the great modern art teachers; he believed that the teacher's task was to set the student free to be himself. Within a brief six years, his classroom produced two major painters, Rouault and Matisse. It also produced four painters who had much to do with the Fauve color revolution of 1905—Albert Marquet, Henri Manguin, Charles Camoin and the Belgian painter Henri Evenepoel. From his classes, too, came Simon Bussy, whose portraits of André Gide and Paul Valéry are the best likenesses ever produced of these two great French writers. At a time when every other teacher on the Beaux-Arts faculty detested his ideas, Moreau was the school's one civilizing influence.

Matisse never forgot his years with Moreau. Years later his eyes would mist over at the mention of his name, and he could draw an exact plan of the classroom from memory—who sat where, what the furniture was like, where the light fell, and so on. Three of his fellow students meant much to him. Simon Bussy, although not a major painter, was a loyal friend to Matisse, one of the few people with whom he kept up a lifelong correspondence. Tiny in stature (he bought all his clothes in a British schoolboys' shop in London), outspoken by nature, Bussy was possessed of a well-stocked and neatly ordered mind. Georges Rouault, a painter of much greater gifts than Bussy, was also important to Matisse. Although he and Matisse were never cut out for close friendship, they always respected one another. Rouault was deeply religious and profoundly concerned with the woes and iniquities of the world. Even in his student days he had a fixity of purpose and a grandeur of imagination that set him apart from his fellows. Rouault saw painting not as a pastime, but as a way of embracing life and reinterpreting it for a public much in need of admonition.

The third member of Moreau's class whom Matisse came to know well was Albert Marquet. He was six years Matisse's junior, but had already had eight years of art training; at 15 he had been admitted to the École des Arts Décoratifs. Marquet had a slightly deformed leg and wore thick, heavy-rimmed spectacles, which set him apart from other boys and gave him a dreadful time in school. Other human beings, it seemed to him, were at best indifferent and at worst actively hostile. In self-defense he had become solitary and withdrawn. As a boy he had wandered alone for weeks on end along the Bordeaux waterfront, sketching everything that caught his fancy. All his life he was a marvelous reporter of what the French call *la chose vue*, the thing seen, the slice of life.

Matisse was then, as he was all his life, a bear for work. There was never anything about him of the easygoing bohemian. But after he met Marquet, the two of them used to go out together in the evenings, along the streets of Paris, covering sheet after sheet of paper with little thumbnail sketches. To Matisse, whose notion of drawing was related exclusively to the sober, concentrated work of the schoolroom, these sketching excursions to the cafés, bars and music halls were invaluable. Neither student had any money to spare, and they made a cup of coffee go a very long way as they sat watching the city's night world, then at its most vivid, and while it eddied round them, put down on paper as much of it as they could.

When Matisse left his bachelor room on the Rue des Écoles, it was either to go to school or to the Louvre or on one of these sketching promenades with Marquet. He had no spare time, in the conventional sense, and all his efforts were directed towards the two days of the week, Wednesday and Saturday, when Moreau corrected his students' work. Not that Moreau was a tyrant: far from it. There was no nonsense about Authority with a capital A, or about Standing with a capital S when he came into the classroom, and his presence was certainly not imposing. One acquaintance, seeing him on the street, observed that he looked like "an obscure country gentleman who had come up to Paris for the horse show." Nevertheless, when he appeared on correction day, wearing his skullcap and dirty white smock, his students were in no doubt about Moreau's ability to judge what was best for each and every one of them.

On some students, Moreau's teaching was wasted. Fewer than one in 10 had any real talent. Those whose names have gone down in history formed a compact group at the back of the room, where the others were less likely to disturb them. The rest were lazy or boisterous or ungifted, or were immature careerists who were "in art" for what they could get out of it. But every one of them, genius or dullard, idler or workhorse, listened carefully when Moreau spoke. Unlike other members of the faculty, whose teaching was based on a fixed hierarchy of values in which their own work stood somewhere near the top, Moreau never mentioned his own paintings. And he was constantly shifting his ground. He took his students to the Louvre as often as possible, and once there kept their imaginations on the move. One day he would speak to them of the glowing colors of the masters of the Italian Renaissance, whose work he knew well from a trip he had taken to Italy in 1857 with Edgar Degas. The next day he would suddenly exclaim, "You know there are times when I'd give everything I possess for one little piece of Rembrandt's mud." He scandalized other faculty members by telling his pupils to get out in the street and study real life, and by encouraging them to go and look at the work of new painters in the galleries. "Don't miss that Toulouse-Lautrec in the Rue Laffitte," he told them one day. "It might have been painted in absinthe."

Matisse was formed by Moreau. One after another of Moreau's remarks can be set, like mottoes, beneath the great paintings of Matisse's maturity. "Nature," Moreau would say, "is simply an opportunity for the artist to express himself." Or again: "*Think* your color! Know how to imagine it!" At a time when most painters were still striving to portray nature objectively, Moreau was suggesting that this was a waste of time. It was useless, he said, to hope for "effects of light" that compared with nature's. Much better to imagine light and imagine color with such intensity that the observer would forget nature and see only the artist's vision of the world. In the words of Rouault, Moreau believed that the exceptional student could be taught to "discipline his will without reference to preconceived method, and to remain true to his inner vision."

Matisse was one of those exceptional students, but he had come late to painting. He was not yet ready to think of putting aside preconceived method. He wanted to learn from the Old Masters, and he wanted to learn from inside: by copying their work. Copying can be a drudgery, but it can also be an adventure in understanding. Matisse chose his models with care. Although he loved the Goya painting of two women in Lille, for instance, and once said of it, "If that's what painting is about, I think I can do it too!", he knew that no beginner could hope to imitate its reckless mastery. The pictures he chose to copy were, for the most part, painstaking reconstructions of everyday life by painters who had tried to set down what they saw as accurately as possible. The Dutch and Flemish masters were his favorites. Much later he spoke of "the scale of silvers and grays, so dear to the Dutch masters, from which I learned to make light sing out in subdued harmonies and to get my values precisely in tune."

Gustave Moreau's class of 1897 poses on the steps of the École des Beaux-Arts for a mock-serious portrait (one student at upper left is solicitously helping the statue blow its nose). Rouault stands, bewhiskered and bareheaded, in the center of the picture. This class was Moreau's last; he died the following year.

Matisse at 26 could scarcely have been taken for either a youthful prodigy or a rebel in the making. He seemed a painter primarily interested in playing off one gray against another. His one painting of any consequence during this period bears this out. It is *Gustave Moreau's Classroom*, a scene very familiar to him and a good subject for a painting. It offered the challenge of the human body, dressed and undressed, the dramatic fall of light from high side-windows, the complex patterning of easels and stools and canvases, and the presence of an occasional antique cast. Matisse did very well with all these things, putting them together in an easy but unconventional relationship. And he maneuvered with great skill between the flesh color of the model's body, the flat white of a plaster cast behind her, the whites and tans of the canvases racked along the wall, the gray of the studio floor and the sharp white of the students' collars. But of Matisse the revolutionary colorist there was, as yet, no trace.

In 1895, Matisse moved downhill from the Rue des Écoles to 19 Quai St.-Michel, a house that stood on the left bank of the Seine with a view downstream to the Louvre and upstream to Notre Dame. His room was high up, near the roof, and his neighbor across the landing was another young painter, Émile Wéry. Wéry was no genius, but he was in touch with things and made it his business to be aware of the new and the novel long before they were much publicized. Matisse and Wéry were each aware of what the other offered, and eventually much good came from their encounter. But for the moment Matisse did not want to be distracted. He had his own self-imposed program, and it was still concerned with the art of the past. In the summer of 1895 he went to the village of Pont-Aven in Brittany, once a favorite spot of Gauguin and his friends. In fact, he even put up at the Pension Gloanec, Gauguin's old headquarters. But instead of being influenced by this, he went ahead patiently and quietly as though Gauguin had never existed, working on the paintings he meant to submit to the Salon of the Société Nationale des Beaux-Arts for exhibit the following spring.

Five of these paintings were accepted by the Salon. This was the first public showing of his work, and the pictures amounted to a catalogue of Matisse's current enthusiasms. In addition to *Gustave Moreau's Classroom*, there were two still lifes, a Breton landscape and a portrait study, *Woman Reading*. Each is signed, as it were, by proxy. The Dutch masters are in the careful plotting of light on jugs and glasses, the French still-life painter Chardin is in the tender fullness of fruits and flowers, Camille Corot is in the tranced and golden light of the Breton landscape. Last but not least, *Woman Reading* is in essence an act of homage to Vermeer's *Lace-Maker*, which Matisse had seen many times in the Louvre.

Two of the paintings, *Woman Reading* and *Still Life with Black Knife*, were sold almost immediately, which must have reassured Matisse's father. *Woman Reading* was even purchased by Félix Faure, president of the French republic, and hung in his private apartment at Rambouillet, the presidential hunting lodge and summer residence just outside Paris. In addition, the eminent art critic Roger Marx liked Matisse's entries well enough to become one of his keen supporters, and Puvis de Chavannes, then one of the most famous painters in Europe, nominated Matisse for permanent membership in the Salon—an honor that carried with it the right to bypass the entrance jury at future Salons. He could hardly, in short, have had a greater success, and he could have had a comfortable life almost for the asking. Roger Marx, for instance, was a member of the committee that purchased copies of Old Masters to be hung in public buildings all over France. He was happy to recommend Matisse for this work, through which Matisse earned as much as 1,200 francs per copy—at a time when a single franc bought a passable dinner. He could also have found plenty of customers for more paintings like *Woman Reading* and *Still Life with Black Knife.*

But it was not enough, and Matisse knew it. In the summer of 1896, almost within days of the Salon's closing, he set out again for Brittany, this time with Wéry at his side. Through Wéry he came to know the Australian Impressionist John Russell, then living at Belle-Île on the Breton coast. Russell was a friend of Monet and Van Gogh, and he often talked to Matisse about them, telling him what they were like, how they persisted in their own work regardless of how others felt about it, how they valued above all else their own unblemished independence; Russell even gave Matisse two Van Gogh drawings. Matisse was too sensitive an artist not to be struck by the difference between the attitude of Monet and Van Gogh and the attitude of the Establishment. There was, however, no immediate change in his own art. Although he did experiment with pure color in one or two small seascapes, laying the color directly onto the canvas in response to his own sensations, Matisse's major painting that summer was *Breton Serving Girl (page 24),* a picture of a young woman in local costume bending over a table laden with bottles, dishes and a loaf of bread. It was, in effect, a Dutch interior transposed into the sharp marine light of Brittany.

Breton Serving Girl was prepared especially for the Salon at a time when people still expected Salon pictures to be carefully worked over, with every inch of canvas filled and a lot going on inside. People lived then in crowded, complicated interiors. The average bourgeois home was packed with silks and brocades and tapestries, with elaborately shaded lamps and tables groaning with knickknacks; there was a real horror of emptiness. Not surprisingly, the ideal Salon picture contained a knight in armor, a group of cardinals, some tropical vegetation, some counterfeit stained glass, a medieval feast with every dish and goblet shown in meticulous detail, a distant view of Constantinople through a window in the background, and in the foreground, three or four naked women, dancing.

Matisse did not go along with this sort of thing wholeheartedly, but he did feel bound to offer a well-furnished picture. *Interior with Top Hat,* painted in the same year as *Breton Serving Girl,* is proof of this. Jan Davidsz. de Heem, the 17th Century Dutch master whose work Matisse often copied, would have admired the sheer variety of objects that Matisse managed to get into this picture. Along with the hat of the title, it contains a desk top heaped with books and papers, porcelain vases of various textures, a lamp, a glass bottle and tumbler, and a wall filled with paintings and picture frames. All of the objects are somehow real and touchable, as if the spectator could reach out and take what he fancied. It is a patient, laborious piece of work.

Sometime in the fall of 1896, Gustave Moreau took Matisse aside and suggested to him that it was high time he risked himself on a big, important painting. There were several reasons for this. Matisse was by now one of the acknowledged leaders in Moreau's class, and Moreau wanted him to prove himself in 19th Century terms. To painters of Moreau's generation—and Moreau was then in his seventies—the decisive test of a painter's ability was the large painting on a large subject. Canvases such as Géricault's *Raft of the "Medusa,"* Delacroix' *Death of Sardanapalus* or Courbet's *The Painter's Studio* were, in effect, ordeals of manhood for their creators—and in pre-Impressionist days the ordeal had been taken for granted. Even when it failed, as it did in Ingres' *Apotheosis of Homer* or Corot's *Homer and the Shepherds*, it had to be attempted. The painter owed it to his public, and to himself.

Moreau's second reason for urging this big picture upon Matisse involved the question of the Prix de Rome. This prize, which still exists, was open to all art students and entitled the winner to study for several years in Rome at the expense of the French government. Lodged, fed and generally looked after in the Villa Medici, one of the world's great houses, winners of the prize had the run of what was then regarded as the supreme repository of Western art. Over and above these material benefits, the Prix de Rome marked a man for life as a person of outstanding gifts. To have won a Prix de Rome gave a young painter a head start over his contemporaries, and if in later life he applied for an academic or government post, "former Rome prizewinner" was the strongest of recommendations. In any case, few young artists dared think of their future in terms that ignored the existence of this official road to success.

Moreau himself did not especially approve of the Prix de Rome competition, and Matisse in later life could scarcely contain himself on the subject. "What makes it so pernicious," he said, "is the preparation for it. It's simply an apparatus for sending the student out of his mind. For one student like Rouault, who had a good head on his shoulders, how many were there who lost the chance of becoming normal citizens and remained ineffectual artists for the rest of their lives!" Nevertheless, Rouault's example may have inspired Matisse to try a man-sized painting of his own. Rouault had tried twice for the Prix de Rome, turning out mammoth Biblical canvases, and both times he had failed. Undeterred, he had gone on to produce, in 1897, a third major painting on a subject of his own invention, *Le Chantier (page 23)*.

Le Chantier, one of the great European paintings, is set in that indeterminate industrial region, neither city nor suburbs, which Frenchmen call *la zone*. It is barely dawn, but already the factories in the distance are in full output, and groups of people in twos and threes are passing across the desolate scene on the way to industrial serfdom. In the foreground two men are fighting fiercely, seemingly to the death, but no one notices and no one cares: the Industrial Revolution has blackened men's hearts as it has blackened the landscape. The whole of Rouault's childhood and youth in the working-class quarter of Paris is in this painting: he meant it as an indictment of society. Moreau, when he saw it, likened its depth and breadth of vision to Shakespeare's historical plays. "In this painting," he said to Rouault, "you are Shakespeare's countryman."

Matisse was impressed by the quality of the effort Rouault had put into this painting, but he knew that he himself was not meant for such themes. His art was then, as it was to remain, entirely without any social or political or religious commitment. Matisse did not aspire to change society, or even to leave a portrait of it. No one ever heard him talk politics, and he lived and died an unbeliever. Even at its most revolutionary, his art was traditional in subject matter: he painted pictures of family life, of tables laden with good things to eat and drink, of beautiful women taking their ease in beautiful surroundings. No one, looking at a Matisse exhibition, would guess that he lived during some of the most terrible years of human history and that the world changed radically and irreversibly during the span of his lifetime. His paintings are, in a sense, portraits of an earthly paradise.

Consequently, when Moreau challenged him to produce a big picture for the 1897 Salon, Matisse turned to one of the great recurrent themes of French painting: *The Dinner Table*. Matisse's table is that of a well-to-do household with a faithful maidservant, familiar to readers of French literature from Molière to Proust. The maid is giving a last touch to the flowers; the silver has been cleaned until it sparkles; the fruit, hand-picked, is piled high in the center of the table; there is red and white wine in abundance. A sense of order and well-being and fastidious opulence pervades the whole scene.

The Dinner Table (pages 24-25) conveys, among other things, the vast improvement in Matisse's technical apparatus. Its many individual still lifes are carried off with a brilliance that makes the *Breton Serving Girl* look timid and stiff. Matisse was also learning how to compose. He knew, for instance, how to keep the picture from straggling away at the edges. The verticals of the decanters are so forthright that, said Moreau, "You could hang your hat on them if you wanted," while the horizontals of dado and picture frame provide a complementary steadying influence. The picture is bolder and firmer than anything Matisse had attempted before. It is also his salute to Impressionism, whose influence he had been able to assimilate in a very short time.

But whatever *The Dinner Table* is, it is above all a farewell. Matisse always seemed to know when he had got all he could out of one way of painting, and he knew when he had finished *The Dinner Table* that he had mastered Impressionism and was ready to move on. Henceforth he would be out on his own. In this context, he was to remember many times Moreau's prophetic statement: "You were born to simplify painting." Working his way toward this goal with characteristic persistence, Matisse eventually produced, in the decade before 1914, the great paintings that proved Moreau to be right.

Henri Matisse was schooled as a lawyer, and did not take up art seriously until his early twenties. But when he did, he pursued his training with the logic and determination of an attorney defending a client. He was sure of what he wanted to do, and he was not afraid to express opinions. On his first morning at the École des Beaux-Arts in Paris, he strode into class with his hat on. When his annoyed teacher objected, Matisse is supposed to have calmly informed him, "I'll take it off as soon as you shut the window. There is a strong draft in here."

Such a demonstrably self-assured man would seem to be equally certain of his artistic goals. But it took Matisse many torturous years to develop his own style. Under the guidance of his teacher Gustave Moreau, at the Beaux-Arts, he gained the fundamentals of drawing and composition; by examining Impressionist paintings he came to understand the intense feeling pure color could convey; from his study of Cézanne he learned that a painting must be solidly constructed. These revelations were the results of years of keen observation and wearying toil—years during which the despairing artist was often on the brink of abandoning painting. Matisse copied museum works, experimented with different styles and wrestled with the concepts of the masters and the moderns. From this quest a new and vital art emerged— an art that appeared deceptively simple, but one that only a passionately dedicated man could have created.

The Late Beginner

The serious and poised Matisse painted this self-portrait in Paris in 1900, when he was 31 years old. He continued to observe and paint himself throughout his life in straightforward self-portraits *(page 81)*, in deft crayon sketches *(page 6)* and as an artist with his model *(pages 110-111)*.

Self-Portrait, 1900

Gustave Moreau: *The Unicorns*, c. 1890

A gifted painter and a superb teacher, Gustave Moreau in the 1890s inspired and guided some of France's finest modern artists, including Matisse, Georges Rouault and Albert Marquet. Moreau's own paintings were traditional in technique but unconventional in content. He followed a rule of "necessary richness," filling pictures like *The Unicorns (left)* with ornate fantasies of elegant maidens and mythological beasts. But as a teacher at the Beaux-Arts, Moreau encouraged simple and colorful pictures, urging his students into the streets to paint what they saw.

Moreau's favorite student was Rouault, a deeply religious man whose early work *(below)* reveals his visceral feeling for the industrial countryside of his youth, with its brutalizing factories and random, vicious fights. Another pupil was Marquet, who was also introspective but to the point of chronic self-depreciation. Overshadowed by Matisse and Rouault, partly because he was so shy, he went unrecognized until late in life, when his modest landscapes and scenes of daily life gained him some fame.

Albert Marquet: *Nude Called Fauve*, 1898

Georges Rouault: *Le Chantier*, 1897

Breton Serving Girl, 1896

Still Life with Fruit Dish, 1897-1898

Matisse gained technical expertise from his studies with Moreau, but outside the classroom he spent lonely hours at his easel desperately trying to assimilate all that he was learning. It was not until he took a summer trip to Belle Isle on the coast of Brittany in 1896, when he was 27, that he first attempted paintings that were more than exercises. One of the finest of these is *Breton Serving Girl (top)*, which shows Matisse's interest in the detail and setting of the Dutch masters. More significantly, at Belle Isle he began to understand the effects of pure

The Dinner Table (or *La Desserte*), 1897

color, as is seen in the luminous still life at left, above.

Matisse's awareness of color was gained at Belle Isle in an entirely unexpected way. He met the painter John P. Russell, who had worked with the great Impressionist Claude Monet. Through Russell's own work and his

collection of modern art—he gave Matisse two drawings by Van Gogh—the artist was liberated from "museum" art. At the urging of Moreau, Matisse in Paris painted *The Dinner Table (above)*, a rich evocation of Impressionism that glows with shimmering colors.

The deliberate Matisse was never stampeded by his own discoveries. His career was a sequence of revelations followed by periods of sober reflection and synthesis. Thus, once he understood the power of pure colors, he resolutely solidified his art by learning to construct a painting exactly. In this he was guided by the work of Cézanne, whose painting *Three Bathers* he kept in his studio for most of his life. So much did Matisse believe in Cézanne's genius that he would constantly remind his friends, "Cézanne is the master of us all."

Male Model, c. 1900

Matisse's *Male Model (below, left)* is clearly in debt to Cézanne, with its angular planes, dark blues and greens, and the solidity of a stone statue. Another nude study, *Carmelina (below, right)* is in many ways a subtler, softer, more mature effort. The essential lesson from Cézanne is not forgotten—the painting has been planned as though by a gifted architect. The sharp planes of Cézanne give way to a sense of roundness, although the colors are still subdued. Soon they would burst out, but Matisse was moving at his own pace toward a personal style.

Carmelina, 1903

II

Experiments with the Dot

Matisse, in March 1897, could be thought to have gotten more than his fair share of the cream. He had an ideally stimulating teacher, he had official recognition as an artist and he had the support of people whose opinions mattered. One of his paintings hung in the country residence of the head of the French state. One of his champions was Puvis de Chavannes, president of the Salon, and another was the influential art critic Roger Marx. His fellow students recognized his extraordinary fixity of purpose and acknowledged him to be their natural leader. Lively and informed people were his friends. Best of all, he had just completed a major painting, *The Dinner Table*, in which he felt that his love for paint and painting had at last paid off.

A month later the cream curdled. When *The Dinner Table* was put on view at the Salon, Matisse found himself, for the first time, under open attack. "You would have thought," said Matisse, referring to the wine carafes in the picture, "that there were microbes at the bottom of all my decanters." The painting was taken as a manifesto for Impressionism, which many people still felt was not respectable. A large group of Impressionist paintings—among them masterpieces by Monet, Renoir and Pissarro—had just been put on show at the Musée du Luxembourg, then France's equivalent of a museum of modern art. The paintings had been left to the museum by a wealthy collector, Gustave Caillebotte, and their display in the museum, long a stronghold of dull and conventional academic art, had aroused a lively controversy. Matisse was suspected of deliberately adding to the fuss by sending a provocative, Impressionist-type painting to the Salon.

This was nonsense in both human and artistic terms. Matisse was not out to make a stir; he was out to explore, one after another, the long-term prospects for painting. Moreau was a great teacher, but there were gaps in his teaching that his students had to fill in for themselves. Cézanne, for instance, was never mentioned in his classroom—and a student who had not come to grips with Cézanne simply was not equipped to cope with the central question of 20th Century painting: "What should a picture be?"

Too poor to hire a professional model, Matisse dressed his wife as a torero for this painting. As he struggled with the work, she grew tired in the awkward position and accidentally plucked the guitar strings. Matisse, angered by the distraction, kicked his easel and sent the painting flying. They both burst into laughter, breaking the tension and enabling Matisse to complete the work.

The Guitarist (Mme. Matisse), 1903

The photograph above was taken at the time
of Matisse's wedding, when, at the age of 29,
he had doubts about continuing his painting,
but not about his decision to marry Amélie
Parayre. She was, to him, "a person of great
kindness, strength and gentleness." Their
wedding took place on January 8, 1898, and
for many years she lavished on Matisse a
devotion that included equal parts of generous
self-sacrifice and the utmost practicality.

Painters have asked themselves this question since the beginning of
time, but around 1900 it had a peculiar complexity. Almost everyone
agreed that the painter was no longer bound to imitate what he saw before him, that it was for him, not nature, to dictate what a painting
should be. He could heighten color, reshape forms, rearrange objects as
he liked. He could add, and he could omit. Once the humble servant of
nature, he could now claim to be nature's rival and equal. But freedom
carries with it the elements of doubt and uncertainty. A man who can
do anything will often find it hard to decide what it is he most wants to
do. For this reason the years between 1900 and 1914 were marked by
an exceptionally rapid turnover in painting styles. What was "in" one
year was "out" the next. For a painter like Matisse, neither young nor
self-assured, the situation was especially difficult.

In any case, the question before Matisse was soon not, "What should
a picture be?" but, "Can I go on painting?" He had been living, up to
this point, on a small allowance from home and the occasional sale of a
painting. But *The Dinner Table* had put people off, and his father was
threatening to discontinue his support. To complicate matters further,
in January 1898 Matisse decided to get married. His wife was Amélie-
Noëlie-Alexandrine Parayre, a beautiful girl from the country near
Toulouse, whom he had met a month or so before at the wedding of mu-
tual friends. Madame Matisse ranks high in the canon of artists' wives.
Matisse loved and prized her for her beautiful dark hair, for her dis-
tinction of carriage, for the way she could carry off all kinds of fancy
dress and for the gaiety with which she lent herself to this studio make-
believe. But within the elegant figure stood fortitude personified. There
was nothing she would not do to help Matisse, and in the difficult years
no one could have been more staunch or resourceful.

After a brief wedding trip to London, Matisse and his bride went on
an extended and economical honeymoon to Corsica. It was February
1899 before they got back to Paris and settled again in the apartment at
19 Quai St.-Michel. Paris, however, was not the same. While they were
gone, Gustave Moreau had died—of the cancer which for some time
had made his life unbearable. His successor at the École des Beaux-Arts
was Fernand Cormon, a painter of popular historical canvases. Cormon
was appalled by Matisse's work in his classroom. "Is that man serious?" he asked. "How old is he?" On learning that the undeniably serious Matisse was going on 30 years old, he sent word that he would
have to give way to a younger student.

Matisse had missed Moreau dreadfully, and now he missed the environment of the school. Private art classes and part-time ateliers were
no substitute. At the Salon he was less and less welcome, for his patron
there, Puvis de Chavannes, had died, and the other members did not
want to be bothered with Matisse's controversial canvases. Paris had become a desert for him. To make even the shadow of a living, he had to
turn to menial work. For months in 1900, for instance, he worked on
the decoration of the Grand Palais, a huge exhibition hall then being
built just off the Champs-Élysées. Much of it was hackwork—gilding a
cornice of laurel leaves, for example—but Matisse did it as conscien-

tiously as he did everything else. His friend Marquet, who was also employed on the job, lacked Matisse's self-discipline. "Just think," he said one morning shortly after they had begun, "another seven hours to go!" To which Matisse replied, "Say that again and I'll kill you!"

The damp and the dust of the half-finished Grand Palais gave Matisse an attack of bronchitis that he could not shake off, and in the spring of 1901 his father took him to Switzerland for a few weeks, hoping the mountain air would cure him. It did, and while there he painted several small-scale landscapes. But the big projects that might have reassured his father were held in abeyance. Despairing once and for all of his son's future as a painter, Émile Matisse finally cut off the small allowance that had been Matisse's main source of support. With not a single patron in sight, and with three small children (Marguerite is now the wife of the art historian Georges Duthuit, Jean is a sculptor and Pierre is the director of a distinguished New York art gallery), Matisse had no choice but to return home to his parents' house at Bohain-en-Vermandois.

The years 1902 and 1903 were a time of dread and dudgeon for Matisse. He hung his pictures in the Salons, but few of them found buyers. He tried to get a small group of admirers to band together and subsidize him, but nothing came of it. His children were periodically farmed out among relatives. If it had not been for the resourcefulness of Madame Matisse, who opened a small hat shop on the Rue de Châteaudun, the household might not have kept going. Yet during this period of extreme crisis, Matisse at last discovered where he wanted to go in painting—and Cézanne showed him the way.

Matisse came to know Cézanne's work through visits to Ambroise Vollard, the great art dealer, who owned Cézannes by the dozens. Behind his apparently pathological sloth—Vollard often fell asleep in the middle of conversations—this curious man had an exceptional business sense. He knew good work when he saw it, and he knew how to bind artists to him hand and foot, buying their paintings when no one else would and putting them under contract. The extent of Vollard's holdings in paintings by Cézanne, Degas, Renoir and others has never been made known—he was secretive about his acquisitions and a haphazard record-keeper. But it is probably safe to say that at the time of his death in 1939, he owned more Impressionist and Post-Impressionist masterpieces than any museum. To step into his little shop was an adventure.

Matisse was introduced to this adventure by Camille Pissarro, an older painter who loved young people and would do anything he could to help them. One day he told Matisse that Cézanne was the man for him to study. Cézanne, he said, was the exact opposite of the Impressionists. Where they set out to capture whatever fleeting effect nature set in their way, Cézanne preferred to leave nothing to chance. He organized his pictures tightly and completely. Every stroke had a meaning, and the meaning was directed and controlled by Cézanne. Matisse had long wanted to follow Moreau's advice to "simplify painting," and now Cézanne showed him how. The secret was to put down on the canvas only those elements that were essential to his own idea.

Matisse is very much the family man in this early snapshot of him, his wife and three children—Pierre, at left; Jean, with a friend perched on his shoulders; and Marguerite. Marguerite was totally devoted to her father and patiently posed again and again for drawings and paintings. The boys, more restless, evaded that task as often as they could, but they too, singly or together, served as models. All the children, with Madame Matisse, appear in the famous Matisse painting, *The Painter's Family (page 87).*

This discovery so haunted Matisse that he felt he had to have a painting by Cézanne continually at hand. Another painter might have settled for a photograph or a print, but not Matisse. In 1899 he managed to scrape together 500 francs for a down payment on a small Cézanne he had seen at Vollard's: *Three Bathers*. It was not always easy to buy from Vollard, who was inclined to say, "I'll think it over," while he multiplied the price by 10. But for once Matisse was lucky, and for 1,500 francs he got not only the Cézanne, but also a small head of a boy by Gauguin and a bust by Rodin. There were to be many moments at which "Sell your Cézanne!" was the advice of friends who saw that the Matisses were near to destitution. But Matisse needed the picture the way a deep-sea diver needs oxygen, and would never be parted from it.

Looking at his later work, it is easy to see why. *Three Bathers* is one of many pictures in which Cézanne tackled the problem of portraying the naked human body in the open air. Most pictures of this sort suggest, even if they don't mean to, that this is an unnatural state of affairs. Cézanne's bathers do not. He managed to make his undressed bodies look as much at home in their setting as the trees and grass, and he did this by treating them simply as objects, no more or less important than anything else in the picture. His bathers have the kind of blundering awkwardness that real people have in such situations, but they also have an unfeigned, organic quality—like the trees and rocks and moving water. The picture is all one, and what makes it all one is the unifying, directing intelligence of the artist.

The first effect of *Three Bathers* upon Matisse was that he decided to restudy the problem of the nude. Cézanne's approach was sculptural in that he wanted to give his figures weight and volume, fullness and roundness. Never one to feign a knowledge he did not possess, Matisse went humbly back to school and learned to do sculpture. Enrolling in the free sculpture classes offered by the École de la Ville de Paris, he worked and worked and worked. When assigned, for instance, to copy a bronze by the French 19th Century animal sculptor A. L. Barye, *Jaguar Devouring a Hare*, Matisse was not content to merely reproduce its exterior, but spent months studying the anatomy of the hare.

His first major piece of sculpture was a standing male nude, *The Serf*. It was inspired by a famous Rodin sculpture, *Man Walking*, and the model who posed for it was a model often used by Rodin, a powerful Italian peasant named Bevilacqua. But as with the Barye sculpture, there was no question of mere imitation. Bevilacqua was a square-built giant of a man with a markedly anthropoid appearance, and Matisse had him pose more than 500 times before he was satisfied. He used those 500 sittings to find out exactly what to emphasize, distort, rearrange and abbreviate in order to capture the essence of the man. The completed work was Bevilacqua, all right, but it was also a fortress—an image of strength and resistance that went far beyond everyday experience.

At the same time Matisse was also painting Bevilacqua, and the brushstrokes he used on this series of male nudes were very different from the delicate, petal-like brushstrokes he had been using on his little

Only when he was old, famous and totally sure of his art could Matisse bear to part with Cézanne's *Three Bathers*, which he had bought from the dealer, Vollard, in 1899. When he presented the small painting to the Petit Palais Museum, he expressed some of the deep feelings that had impelled him to purchase it originally and keep it close to him through all the subsequent years: "I have owned this canvas for 37 years. . . . It has sustained me spiritually in the critical moments of my career as an artist; I have drawn from it my faith and my perseverance."

landscapes. The nudes look as though they had been hewn out of stone with a chopper. Matisse would dent the figure beneath the left breast, for instance, like a wounded warrior, or scar and slash the forms of the body, emphasizing them to the point of parody. He would examine those forms under strong light that was by turns white, purple, ginger-red and greeny-blue. In short, he was wrestling with the lessons of Cézanne and Rodin as Jacob had wrestled with the angel.

In 1901 he turned to the female nude and again went all out for power and monumentality and strange, arresting colors. Although he did not dig into the living flesh as he had done with the male nudes, he did break through to a quite new intensity of expression. He would put the model, for instance, against an orange background and draw in her nose and eyebrow in one unbroken sickle-shaped line. It was a line that had nothing to do with the "good painting" of the academy, and nothing to do with actual experience. And yet, for all that, it was manifestly right. It recorded the experience of looking at a naked woman more directly and more vividly than art had ever done before. What normally comes quilted and felted and wrapped in asbestos is here branded upon the senses with a red-hot iron.

Painting of this kind puts a tremendous strain upon the artist. Matisse always appeared to be the most circumspect of men, but actually he worked in an atmosphere of intense and lasting anguish. At the easel he often showed all the physical symptoms of extreme fear: he trembled, wept, cursed, broke out into torrential sweats and was subject to impulses of unaccountable violence. His son-in-law Georges Duthuit once wrote that "Matisse knew many a moment of panic. His evolution did not by any means go forward in a blaze of light. It was not an uninterrupted mystical ascension. Nor did he ever burn himself out in a single burst of flame. He progressed toward an idea of reality that was

Turning to sculpture in a deepening exploration of the human form, Matisse in 1900 began work in clay on a piece called *The Serf* at his Paris studio *(left)* on Quai St.-Michel. Matisse aimed to simplify, eliminating everything extraneous to the essential qualities of a subject. To reach that goal, he heeded the great Rodin's advice that a sculptor should consider each element of the human body as a separate unit: in the final version of this first sculpture, *The Serf (above)*, completed in 1903, Matisse omitted as superfluous to the expressiveness of the figure the arms that appeared in the study.

constantly being revised. Flights into the empyrean alternated with periods of doubt and darkness in which he needed, as it were, to reassure himself that the earth was still there."

Put in plain words, Matisse suffered when he painted, and he often sought relief in more routine kinds of work. Paris in those days had many small art schools, and he took to dropping in on their classes—much as a prima ballerina at the height of her career still goes to class every morning and slaves among the beginners at the *barre*. His journeys in the course of a day might take him all over Paris, from a private art school in the Rue de Rennes to the Académie Colarossi, then back again after dinner to the municipal sculpture school in the Rue Étienne Marcel. In class he would work patiently at the assigned task, keeping the model in one pose long after the other students had tired of it. When correction time came, the teacher—who might be someone like Eugène Carrière, a painter of sentimental mothers and children—was often appalled by what Matisse was doing, but he could not help being awed by his tenacity of purpose.

A man can be very tenacious indeed and still be grateful for a friend who shares his ideas. In March 1901 Matisse found such a friend. At a retrospective exhibit of Van Gogh's work at the Galerie Bernheim-Jeune, he fell into conversation with André Derain and Maurice Vlaminck. The two men were close friends and neighbors, and they made a spectacular pair. Both were huge, and both wore strange and conspicuous clothes—one of Vlaminck's favorite articles of costume was a painted wooden necktie. In the euphoria of seeing so many paintings by an artist who meant so much to all of them, Derain and Vlaminck pressed Matisse to come back with them to Chatou, the waterside suburb where they lived. Thus began one of the most fruitful associations in modern French art. With Derain, and to a lesser extent with Vlaminck, Matisse went on to break through, in 1905, to the triumph of color for color's sake and the movement called *Fauvism*.

It was a novel experience for Matisse to be with gifted painters who were obviously of a younger generation. "Matisse came down to see us," Vlaminck said of this visit, "and he went home ten years younger!" In a sense it was true. Matisse at the time was 31 and Derain was only 21. As for Vlaminck, although at 25 he was already married and the father of two children, he rarely had two sous to rub together and he took life a great deal more lightly than Matisse had ever done. This was partly a matter of physical type. Vlaminck was a red-headed colossus, well known as a boxer and wrestler, with a superabundant energy that carried him unscathed through adventures that would have prostrated Matisse. He supported himself and his family with seasonal jobs as a violinist—sometimes posing as a gypsy—and by writing pulp novels that skirted the frontiers of pornography.

Vlaminck never thought of his painting as a means of making a living, much less as work that might one day enter a museum. The idea of being a professional painter was, in fact, abhorrent to him. As for establishing some sort of relationship with the great painters of the past, this seemed to him an occupation both pretentious and foredoomed.

"What do I care what other people have done?" he would say. "In art, every generation has to begin all over again for itself." Vlaminck painted the way he felt—directly and without preliminaries. He used pure color, straight from the tube, and made no pretense of drawing. "Our painting," he said later, describing this approach, "was not an invention but an attitude. It was a way of being or acting, of thinking, of breathing. . . ." He instinctively used colors that stood at the very top of the register, and he used them with the kind of abandon that is found in children's art. Early Vlamincks look, in fact, like the work of a talented eight-year-old.

Matisse was fascinated to discover that Vlaminck had arrived, by sheer force of instinct, at the same feeling for the role of color that he, Matisse, had reached through conscious effort and adjustment. Even so, it was not with Vlaminck that he became intimate, but with Derain. Derain's painting at this time was an ambitious, painstaking, low-keyed derivation of Cézanne. Unlike Vlaminck, who claimed to despise intellectual pursuits, Derain read enormously on a wide variety of subjects and knew a great deal about the history of art. At the same time, he could match Vlaminck's rough talk when he wanted to, and he was Vlaminck's equal in physical strength: Derain thought nothing of bicycling 100 miles a day.

Derain and Vlaminck were classic outsiders. In the winter they camped out in an abandoned riverside restaurant, burning its furniture for warmth; in good weather they toured the countryside, alone or in the company of a motley group of bohemians and bums. But there was a difference between them. Vlaminck's parents lived a life scarcely less precarious than his own, while Derain's father was a prosperous Chatou dairyman with a shop on the town square and a seat on the municipal council. Vlaminck often called Derain, half in resentment, half in admiration, "a hot-house plant," and it did not surprise him when Derain's father forbade his son to bring Vlaminck to the house.

At 18, while Vlaminck was batting around the countryside like a buccaneer in search of his prey, Derain was a serious art student, patiently copying Ghirlandaio's *Christ Carrying the Cross* in the Louvre. When Vlaminck went off to serve his time in the army, he treated the whole thing as a frolic—playing cymbals in the regimental band and contributing articles on army life to an anarchist newspaper; Derain detested every moment he spent in the service and could hardly wait to get out.

Vlaminck went for painting as mindlessly as a bull goes for a matador; to Derain painting was part of the whole world of ideas. He had read widely in physics and philosophy, in poetry and art history, and he knew that old ideas about the nature of the universe and the forces within it were being rejected on every hand. It was a time for new, fearless, radical investigations. Derain did not see why painting should be exempt from this. In the winter of 1901, writing to Vlaminck from the north of France in the midst of his military service, Derain observed prophetically, "As for painting, I realize that the period of realism is over. Where painting is concerned, we're only beginning."

Derain's turn of mind was particularly congenial to Matisse. Derain in his way was a universal man: he would have liked to leave his mark upon many spheres of activity—on the theater, on philosophy, on literature, even perhaps on politics—whereas Matisse was only and solely interested in art. But when Derain put aside physics, metaphysics and the ethics of colonial government, and got down to the problems of painting, his thoughts and Matisse's had a way of running parallel. Derain reached, quite on his own, the basic premise of 20th Century art: that painting should offer an equivalent of nature, not an imitation of it. "The great mistake that painters have made," he wrote, "is to have tried to render momentary effects of nature. It has never struck them that what makes these effects has nothing to do with what makes a good painting."

To Derain, a good painting gave the viewer the same sense of heightened vitality that he got from looking at nature—and it was the vitality, not the mimicry, that counted. The painter's job was to find a way of putting down color so that it would act directly upon the viewer's nervous system. To do this, he had to be willing to abandon a large part of the unwritten contract that had hitherto existed between the painter and his audience. According to this contract, the visual experience offered by the painter was supposed to approximate to the visual experience offered by nature. The closer the painting came to this, the more successful it was. Now this familiar experience was about to be changed. And nothing summed up the change more concisely than a remark Matisse made to someone who complained that Matisse had never seen women like the ones he painted. "I don't paint women," Matisse replied, "I paint pictures." Henceforth the picture was an object in its own right, independent of the object that inspired it, subject only to laws of its own making.

Matisse had actually come close to this kind of painting in the winter when he was struggling with the lessons of Cézanne. But characteristically he was slow to make up his mind. For the moment he tacked this way and that, sometimes letting his painting hand run free, sometimes producing work that was almost Germanic in its careful workmanship. These shifts in style could have been due to his private distress over money matters and the dreariness of his life in Bohain-en-Vermandois, where he was forced to spend so much of his time in the winters of 1902 and 1903.

In general, however, Matisse disdained to let his inner feelings show. No one could have guessed, for example, that the dazzling picture he painted of Madame Matisse as *The Guitarist (page 28)* in 1903 was anything but the work of a happy man. He posed his wife in a straight-backed chair, dressed her in a pseudo-Spanish costume that set off her dark southern beauty, gave her a guitar to pluck—or feign to pluck—placed her against a brightly patterned quasi-Spanish backdrop and added some yellow flowers in a crystal vase. In its use of black to accent Madame Matisse's costume it echoed the lustrous black accents used by Manet, and the pose of a woman bent over a guitar harked back to the young woman lutanist of Vermeer's *The Love Letter*. Technically the picture is brilliant, but Matisse in later years remembered it as

Robust, individualistic Maurice Vlaminck—shown here in middle age with his pipe and huge palette—had a passion for painting but did not seriously begin until he met André Derain, with whom he shared a ramshackle studio. "To be a painter," he said, "is not a business, any more than to be an anarchist, lover, racer, dreamer or prizefighter."

being a very fidgety picture to paint, one that he produced under great tension every step of the way.

In the spring of 1904, Matisse received an invitation from the painter Paul Signac to spend the summer with him at St.-Tropez, and the five years of apparently directionless work came to an end. It was as if Matisse had been waiting for something to happen, as if he knew something important was on its way. He longed for someone to talk to, to argue with, and Signac was to be that much-needed person.

Signac was six years older than Matisse, just old enough to have been around in the 1880s when Georges Seurat brought a new kind of painting to Paris. Signac never forgot and never recovered from, the impact of Seurat's *Bathing Place, Asnières (pages 42-43)*. The painting shows a group of young working-class Frenchmen amusing themselves by the Seine during their luncheon break. Some are in the water, some are on the bank; in the distance are the factories to which they will presently return. It is the most ordinary of scenes, yet Seurat has raised it to the level of epic, partly by endowing the individual figures with a monumental grandeur, partly by employing a new painting technique. It was called Pointillism, or Divisionism, or Neo-Impressionism, and it consisted of a novel brushstroke and a completely scientific use of color. Every color was applied in exact lozenge-shaped dots, and every color was accompanied by its complementary color—the one that brought it out, raised it to its maximum strength. Seurat developed his technique in reaction to what seemed to him the aimlessness of Impressionism, and during his short life—he died at 31 of an undiagnosed illness—he used it to paint some of the greatest and most completely successful pictures in European art.

But Seurat's paintings do not owe their greatness to Pointillism alone. He had a superfine social sense and a gift for composition such as occurs only once or twice every hundred years. In a painting like *Sunday Afternoon on the Island of La Grande Jatte (page 44)*, with its characters drawn from every rung on the social ladder, Seurat presented a whole society with the assurance of a Tolstoi or a Balzac. He knew how to mingle high art and low, was as fascinated by billboards as by the pictures in the Louvre. In paintings like *The Parade (page 44)*, with its friezelike panorama of performers and spectators, he put the two kinds of art together. Above all, Seurat had a supreme gift for the memorable image. His paintings are full of things that once seen are never forgotten. One knows all about the young workmen in *Bathing Place, Asnières*, and not only about these particular young men, but about all young men who are the prisoners of an industrial society.

Paul Signac knew that when Seurat died, something irreplaceable had died with him, and he felt it his duty to bear witness to what he had seen. Signac himself was no genius, but he had been close enough to Seurat to study his methods minutely. He came to think, more and more, that Seurat's technique was the natural culmination of a process that had been going on all during the 19th Century. Delacroix, around 1820, had begun to break down his colors in such a way that, when looked at from a distance, they blended with a new intensity. More

André Derain was the son of a prosperous baker who wanted him to follow a respectable career, preferably engineering. The young painter met enormous family opposition to his vocation until Matisse spoke so glowingly of Derain's talent and future prospects that the parents finally gave in, allowed Derain to devote himself to art.

recently the Impressionists had been groping in the same direction when they realized that shadows could be rendered in pure color instead of in terms of a negative near-darkness. Seurat had given these color experiments scientific validity. Seurat's painting was not at all like the painting of the past; it was patient and persnickety, and fine frenzied brushstrokes played no part. But Signac thought Seurat's method was, at the very least, the transitional step to the future.

Undeterred by the fact that no one but Seurat had ever made a total success of Pointillism, Signac set out to publicize it. He talked about it incessantly to everyone within earshot, and in 1899 he published a book about it, *From Delacroix to Neo-Impressionism*. It is a book powered by confidence in the future, addressed to "those who will not be content to do over again what has been done already, but who will have the perilous honor of creating a new way of painting and expressing an ideal that is theirs alone." Something of Signac's optimism must have brushed off on his readers, for the book was widely read and widely talked about. Undoubtedly one of its readers was Matisse, who always kept up with the new in art, and who must have been especially struck by its closing lines: "The triumphant colorist has only to appear: we have prepared his palette for him."

When Signac invited Matisse to St.-Tropez for the summer he probably had in mind to gain a new and important convert. The visit was attractive to Matisse, who was keenly interested in Signac's ideas. In addition, there would be the color and light of the south, which he had missed during the long northern winter, and there would be freedom from money worries. Signac was well off; he owned a villa that dominated the old town of St.-Tropez and was an experienced yachtsman, with a passion for ships and the sea. Altogether the proposal was very appealing. Years later Matisse often spoke of the incongruities of this summer. "It didn't suit me at all," he would say. Not only Signac, but a whole group of Signac's friends and neighbors, were devotees of the dot and of the scientific application of color. For Matisse, who had spent years learning all manner of subtle and unusual color combinations, such servitude was unthinkable. "I could not live," he said later, "among all those provincial aunts."

Yet the following fall, when he got back to Paris, he spent much of his time on a canvas done in the Pointillist style. And Signac, when he saw it at the 1905 Salon des Indépendants, lost no time in buying it. *Luxe, Calme et Volupté (pages 46-47)* is a very odd sort of picture. Its title is taken from a poem by Baudelaire, "L'Invitation au Voyage," about a journey to an imaginary city where cares are unknown and people lead a life of pure pleasure in conditions of luxury and refinement. All this is very different from Matisse's painting. The images in the poem call to mind a room in some Eastern city; Baudelaire speaks of well-waxed furniture and mysterious perfumes, rooftops shimmering under a humid sky, ships at anchor in nearby canals. Matisse's painting is set in the open air; somewhere by the shores of a southern sea, a group of naked women are whiling away the day.

Luxe, Calme et Volupté seems to derive on one hand from the dé-

jeuners sur l'herbe, the Impressionists' "picnics on the grass," at which the ladies present happen to have taken off their clothes. It also seems to derive from Puvis de Chavannes' paintings of an imaginary island of the blest where nobody has to work and nobody is ever ill. Matisse's island of the blest is curiously pinched, however. The vegetation is sparse and spikey, and life looks neither rich nor easy; it is an idyll that generates the least idyllic of feelings—a certain general discomfort. Evidently Matisse was working against his own nature. Pointillism's dot ruled out the unpredictable strokes of color that marked his other landscapes of this period—color that he often placed with all the assurance of a tennis champion putting the ball where it is least expected.

Pointillism also ruled out the passionate, truth-at-any-cost modeling that Matisse had used in his studio nudes of the winter of 1900-1901. That kind of modeling was out of the question when the brush had to stop and start every half-inch. Instead, in *Luxe, Calme et Volupté*, Matisse turned to quite another way of indicating the curves of the human body, one based on the decorative serpentine line of Art Nouveau. It was a line then very much in fashion. Lampstands, inkwells, ashtrays, subway stations and drawings of famous actresses on the covers of theater programs were all being shaped according to Art Nouveau. But the line was not natural to Matisse, and the effort showed.

Luxe, Calme et Volupté was also Matisse's first and last attempt to compose as Seurat had composed. Seurat, in his paintings, had dictated to nature, making it subordinate to design. If he wanted flags to wave in a certain way, they did so—regardless of the direction of the wind; if he wanted a ship's sails to be rigged in a certain way, they were so rigged —even if no such ship had ever put to sea; if he wanted a line of clouds to echo the line of a path along the face of a cliff, the clouds were so arranged—regardless of meteorology. Seurat was also fond of setting up echoes in a picture—of repeating, for instance, the same arabesque line. In *The Circus* the sinuous curve of the ringmaster's whip is repeated in the taut curves of the acrobat's body; in *Le Chahut (The High Kick)*, the upraised arm of the music-hall conductor is repeated in the upward sweep of the dancers' skirts; in *Young Girl Powdering Herself*, the carved detail on a table leg is repeated in the scalloped edge of the girl's bodice.

Seurat managed to build these artificial devices of color, technique and composition into pictures that were at once untrue to nature and intrinsically true to life. Every city park on a summer Sunday has something in it of *La Grande Jatte*. Matisse, never one to abandon a project, had tried to do the same. But the more he tried, as he took *Luxe, Calme et Volupté* from oil-sketch to finished painting, the less plausible it looked. The painting was a success when it was shown at the Salon des Indépendants—and, in fact, it may have attracted more young painters to Pointillism than Signac's book on the subject—but for Matisse Pointillism was a false trail. In the summer of 1905, when Derain got out of the army, the two friends headed south to the fishing village of Collioure, where Matisse was to get back to the kind of work that was to make him, before long, a key figure in European painting.

Making a Science of Art

During the last half of the 19th Century, Darwin and Wallace promulgated the theory of evolution, Pasteur proved that bacteria caused disease and Edison switched on the electric light. The advances in science stimulated a young artist named Georges Seurat to try to achieve through logic what his predecessors, the Impressionists, had done by instinct and emotion: to capture in paint the purity of nature's colors; he wanted to replace Impressionism's subjectivity with an objective record of reality. Studying the theories of chemists and physicists, Seurat worked out divisionism, or Pointillism—a system of stippling the canvas with individual dots of pure, complementary colors—red and green, for example. He did not mix pigments on a palette or combine them with his brush on the canvas, for he believed that the small dots, each the same size, laid precisely side by side, would combine themselves to reproduce the full range of natural colors in the viewer's eye. Later Seurat made the system seem even more scientific by adding geometric rules.

Seeming to offer a new orderliness in painting, Pointillism attracted another young artist, Paul Signac, who undertook to explain Seurat's theories in print. In 1904, 13 years after Seurat's death, Signac introduced Pointillism to Matisse. The orderly-minded Matisse experimented with the method but soon discarded it; he was too imaginative an artist to be restricted by rules in his preoccupation with the relationship of colors.

Signac's lithograph advertising the avant-garde Théâtre-Libre (hence the letters "T-L") is also a demonstration of Pointillist theory. Running up and down the letters and throughout the double borders are pure colors arranged in a sequence devised by Charles Henry, an esthetician-mathematician whose theories of color-contrast and harmony greatly influenced the Pointillists. In the circular painting at the center, Signac's dots demonstrate another of Henry's ideas on color interactions: the spectator's hair changes color as it appears against the background of the stage, the footlights and his own neck.

Paul Signac: *Application du Cercle Chromatique de Mr. Ch. Henry*, 1888-1889

41

Georges Seurat, who introduced some of his theories with this monumental picture, was a shy young man who was willing to lead a revolution in painting. Perhaps he would also have led a social revolution, for his circle of friends consisted of some of the most radical artists and writers of the time. Although Seurat never spoke of his political beliefs, this painting, so widely admired on purely artistic grounds, may reveal some of his feelings. For instance, the small figures on the boat flying the French flag could represent Seurat's view of the current French government, a government that, like the figures, had turned its back on the workers trying to find a little recreation on the shore in the foreground.

Whether or not the painting has a message, it displays Seurat's genius for color and composition. In it, Seurat had not yet fully developed his technique of the dot brushstroke, but his concern with the precise application of color is evident. The superbly disciplined placement of the figures leads the eye across the foreground and into the distance, and light balances shade to achieve a subtle harmony. Indeed, when Signac saw the picture, he sensed that he was in the presence of a masterpiece and he spent the rest of his life working for a broader appreciation of Seurat and his remarkable technique.

42

Georges Pierre Seurat: *Bathing Place* (or *Bathing Party*), *Asnières*, 1883-1884

Although the two Seurat paintings below may seem more poetic than scientific, they illustrate Pointillism's calculations of color and line. The upper picture, which measures just over 10 feet across, is dotted with colors that Seurat had meticulously preselected from a chart constructed according to principles established by the chemist M. E. Chevreul. And the poignancy of the lower picture comes out of geometry as well as genius: the relationship between the vertical and horizontal lines of the painting follows the formulas of Charles Henry, who hypothesized that certain linear combinations produce specific emotions in the observer—a horizontal with

Georges Pierre Seurat: *Sunday Afternoon on the Island of the Grande Jatte,* 1884-1886

Georges Pierre Seurat: *Invitation to the Sideshow* (or *La Parade*), 1887-1888

downward verticals for sadness, a horizontal with upward verticals for gaiety.

Henry's theories are also demonstrated in the witty and energetic portrait below. Painted by Signac, the picture's geometric background of flowers, circles, swirls and waves runs the gamut of emotion-producing lines that Henry claimed to have measured by mathematical equation.

The subject of the picture is Félix Fénéon. Fénéon was an influential and intellectual writer who became an intimate friend of the leading Pointillists and was their dedicated spokesman for many years.

Paul Signac: *Portrait of Félix Fénéon, against Enamel, of a Background Rhythm with Beats and Angles, Tones and Colors,* 1880

Among the many reasons Matisse discarded
Pointillism the same year he adopted it was the matter
of its brushstrokes—the dots or tiny dabs that seemed,
to Signac and others, the only proper way to apply color
to canvas. The technique appeared to serve at least two
purposes. One was practical; at normal viewing distance
the small dots of pure color will begin to blend in the
viewer's eye to become a wide range of vibrating tones
and shapes. (Hold this page close up and then look at it
from several yards' distance to see the difference.) The
other function was less pragmatic: the Pointillists
apparently felt that impersonal, almost mechanical
brushstrokes preserved the scientific integrity of their
work. Neither reason was convincing to Matisse. He
tried to adapt himself to the method but found that he
could no more curb his brush to conform to arbitrary
laws of optical mixture than he could contain his sense
for color within "scientific" guidelines. In the autumn
of 1904, following a summer spent with Signac in the
south of France, he came as close as he could to
orthodox Pointillism by painting the picture shown
here. Despite the haunting quality he achieved, he felt
inhibited by the Pointillist technique all the time he
was working, and the completed picture never pleased
him. Shortly after it was publicly shown (and bought
by Signac), Matisse went back to his own search for a
style. But for the rest of his life he could be grateful to
the Pointillists, for in their own struggle with the new,
they had helped to liberate him from tradition. On his
own he would proceed to a great exploration of color.

46

Luxe, Calme et Volupté, 1904-1905

47

48

III

Among the "Wild Beasts"

Matisse, in the spring of 1905, was 35 years old and had still to produce a painting of which it could be said unequivocally, "This is by Matisse and owes nothing to anyone else." He had, to be sure, produced many beautiful paintings, but they were all in the style of others. He was rather like a particularly conscientious executor, winding up the estates of his predecessors—of Cézanne, of the Impressionists, of Seurat and his friends. So far he had not ventured very far out on his own. Within the next few years, all this was to change. By the spring of 1908 he would be an international art figure, with a school and many eager disciples, and would have signed his name to paintings that are now 20th Century classics.

The beginnings of this change date from the day in the summer of 1905 when Matisse, in company with his friend André Derain, left Paris for the fishing village of Collioure, near the Spanish border. The choice of Collioure as a summer place had been made by Madame Matisse, who had scouted the little town the previous fall. With its harbor full of sailboats, its watchtowers and 17th Century fortifications, its color-washed houses of red, yellow and blue, Collioure could have been relentlessly picturesque. It was saved from this by a hard masculine line, by a functional tautness in the silhouette of battlement and fortress. Signac, who had painted Collioure in 1887, made it look like what it was—a muscular town with the shoulders of a fullback. Now, 18 years later, Matisse and Derain found it an ideal setting in which to pursue a bold new style of painting.

Meanwhile, they came to know each other better. Matisse discovered that Derain moved easily in the world of ideas, and was as ready to talk music or theater or philosophy as he was to argue—for the 500th time —the nature of the "new painting." Derain found Matisse "much more extraordinary than I expected, especially when it comes to clear thinking and psychological speculation." Temperamentally the two were poles apart. Derain rushed at things; Matisse took his time. Their bags were scarcely unpacked before Derain was writing Vlaminck of a complete change in his work; Matisse, however, continued to struggle doggedly with Seurat's dot. French painting at that moment was dominated by this dot, and both Matisse and Derain had tried their hand at it. But the very action of applying the dot, over and over again, was unnatural to men who instinctively used the brush in a very different way. For Matisse, there was one other insuperable objection. From a distance, the complementary dots of intense color merged into half-tones.

Around this time, by happy accident, Derain and Matisse were taken to visit Daniel de Monfreid, a painter who had been a close friend of Gauguin and who owned a number of Gauguin's Tahitian paintings. Matisse had known about Gauguin for years, and had even purchased one of his portraits from Ambroise Vollard. Now, at this crucial moment in his career, Gauguin was at his shoulder, telling him things he needed to hear. Color, Gauguin seemed to say, was as one felt it to be, not as it actually was. He also seemed to say that no art can be great when the forces within a painting neutralize one another—as Seurat's colored dots did.

Matisse went away from Monfreid's house determined to bring new meaning to Signac's famous prediction, "The triumphant colorist has only to appear. We have prepared his palette for him." Instead of applying his colors in well-regulated dabs, he let them rip across the canvas in whatever way suited the picture. In one famous painting from this period, *Landscape at Collioure*, the tree trunks are brushed on in a serpentine line, sometimes broken, sometimes continuous. Their colors, as described by Alfred Barr, are "as one reads the picture from left to right . . . blue-green, maroon, bright blue, yellow-green, scarlet and purple, dark green and violet, and, at the right, ultramarine. They spring from a ground that is spotted blue, orange, ocher and sea-green, and they carry foliage of vermilion, green and lavender. Only the sea in the distance and the sky retain their natural color."

It could have been a mess, but it wasn't. Matisse may have ignored nature's colors, but he kept his own color sense intact. Every touch of color, no matter how arbitrary in itself, was related to every other

Matisse drew *The Fisherman*, the pen-and-ink sketch of the curving beach at right, in 1905, when he and the painter Derain spent the summer in the little fishing port of Collioure. Derain is the faintly seen figure swimming merrily in the cove beyond the patient angler. One of dozens of paintings and drawings that Matisse made at Collioure during the many summer months he spent there, this amusing sketch was later a gift of the artist to his generous Russian patron, Shchukin.

touch. Also, Matisse was helped by the natural quality of Collioure's light. Unlike the light of northern France, which casts deep shadows, the light at Collioure is intense, blonde and all-powerful; it bathes everything in a kind of diffused radiance. To capture this quality in his painting, Matisse left parts of his canvas untouched, and the pure white —along with suggesting intense sunlight—also held the bold colors in balance.

In the fall, back in Paris, Matisse used this new approach to color in a portrait of Madame Matisse that was to become one of the most famous paintings of the century, *Woman with the Hat (page 48)*. Basically the painting was the standard upper-bourgeois portrait of the day. Matisse chose the same pose, the same spectacular hat, the same look of supercilious boredom that marked portrait after portrait in the Salon. But he treated the human face in *Woman with the Hat* exactly as he had treated the Collioure landscape—he rearranged its color structure to suit himself. A broad green stripe ran across the forehead and another went down the bridge of the nose; one cheek was yellowish-green and the other was pinkish-red. But when all these unrealistic patches were put together the end product was a portrait more real than many a naturalistic portrait. The virtuoso color was not merely decorative, still less was it color according to theory; it was color in support of the picture's meaning—it conveyed the festive message fundamental to such "society" portraits.

Woman with the Hat was a true portrait, but the Parisian public of 1905 did not think so. When it was exhibited at the Salon d'Automne of that year, along with four other Matisse canvases, there was a public outcry. People felt that the picture was not simply bad or incomprehensible, but that it was a deliberate insult: it violated not only the sitter's appearance but also the audience's concept of womanhood. They felt the public was being hoaxed and vilified by a painter who ought by rights to have come round, hat in hand, seeking its favor. Painters, at the turn of the century, were regarded almost as civil servants. The painter who made his annual obeisances at the Salon, who kept in touch with the whims of public taste, might hope for steady preferment of the kind enjoyed by members of the Church or the armed services. The Salon was the place where reputations were made or destroyed: trial by public opinion was a fact of life, and the dragon of public disapproval still had all its teeth.

Matisse's *Woman with the Hat* was not, as it happened, the only painting that went beyond the sedate norms of the 1905 Salon. During the previous summer a number of other painters had also been experimenting aggressively with color, sometimes as a group, sometimes in isolation. Derain's friend Vlaminck was one of the experimenters; Henri Manguin, Charles Camoin and Matisse's old schoolmate Albert Marquet were others. At the same time, Rouault, although relatively subdued in color, was startling people with the ferocity of his subject matter—grotesque portraits of circus folk and the demimonde. There was no concerted *putsch* in the work of these men, but the Salon made it seem so by hanging all their pictures together in one room, Room

VII. And the hatred of visitors to Room VII was so intense that the existence of the movement, as a movement, soon became a matter of legend.

The movement was called Fauvism, from an incident often described, and just as often disputed. There was in Room VII a small, conventional statuette of a cupid, done in quasi-Renaissance style by some would-be Donatello whose name is now forgotten. The critic Louis Vauxcelles is said to have walked into Room VII and, noting the discrepancy between statue and paintings, cried, "Aha, Donatello among *les fauves* [wild beasts]!" The name stuck and came to be applied not only to the painters in Room VII but to all painters—among them Braque and Dufy—who were attracted to unrepressed color. Matisse, as the oldest and most publicly reviled, was their acknowledged leader. Within a month or two, his measured and purposeful way of expressing himself had made him, almost in spite of himself, the accredited ambassador of a new way of painting.

"Color for color's sake," a phrase originated by Derain, applied equally to all the Fauves. All of them stood for exhilaration: "Have a good time!" was their message.

In Paris, despite the furor over Fauvism, the idea of enjoying color went down very well, for Paris had always regarded art as a fundamentally comfortable activity. But serious painters were coming up in other places for whom painting was not a superior distraction. "Color for heaven's sake" would have better described the attitude of some of these painters—men who used color to heighten man's sense of his mystical union with the universe—while "color for pity's sake" came closer to the mark for those who used color to awaken man to the wrongs in his own society. The message of the latter painters was not a shout of exhilaration but a cry of protest and pain. It was a cry that ran through the music and literature of central Europe in the years before 1914, as well as through its painting. It was the cry of men who felt themselves dispossessed of the things that should have been theirs by nature.

In art, the great progenitor of this movement, which came to be called Expressionism, was the Norwegian painter Edvard Munch. Munch was six years older than Matisse but had grown up in a very different world. In Oslo it was possible to go to jail simply for expressing unpopular points of view. In 1886 the writer Hans Jaeger was imprisoned, for instance, for publishing an autobiographical novel that acknowledged the existence of sex. Munch was close in spirit to the dramatists Henrik Ibsen and August Strindberg, the latter of whom once described Munch as "the esoteric painter of love, jealousy, death and sadness." Like them, he saw established society as fundamentally evil: mankind was perverted by the demands made upon it by society, and for those who rejected those demands punishment was inevitable.

Compared to the carefree world of the Impressionists—the luncheons out-of-doors where everyone has enough to eat and drink, the dances where everyone has a partner, the sailing parties where the wind never drops and no one is ever seasick—Munch's world is not agreeable. In Munch's paintings physical love is foredoomed by treachery or impotence, death and disease lie in wait for the unblemished body of every young girl, and every evening out is followed by its retributive hangover. Munch could not paint a crowd scene without suggesting that at any moment the crowd might be cut down by cavalry; he could not paint a love scene without suggesting that fate would shortly tear the lovers apart; he could not paint a single figure in a room without suggesting desertion. This was the world Munch saw about him, and it was also the world of his own private experience. His life was one of loneliness, vagabondage and mental breakdown.

In 1893, while Matisse was still a student in Moreau's classroom, Munch was painting the great picture that prefigures the 20th Century's preoccupation with *angst*—the unfocused anguish that poisons the wells of the inner life. *The Cry* shows a dreamlike figure running along a jetty toward the viewer. The mouth, the head, the sea behind it, the clouds and the horizon are all so distorted that finally the whole world seems to be hallooing in fear and agony. Color, in this tormented scene, is the henchman of the artist's thought. "Above the blue-black fiord hung the clouds, red as blood, red as tongues of fire," wrote Munch of the picture's making. "Alone, trembling with anguish, I became aware of the vast, infinite cry of Nature."

At the turn of the century this cry was heard all over Europe. People felt instinctively that terrible times were coming and that nothing could be done about it. Private misfortunes were seen as metaphors for an approaching collective disaster that would put an end forever to the old familiar ways of life. Taboos that had held fast for generations were suddenly seen as degrading; "pillars of society" were derided as hypocrites, and the very notion of authority was considered offensive to free men. All over Europe huge armies were massing, and ingenious weaponry pointed to dreadful conflicts that could not long be delayed. Strikes, assassinations, popular uprisings, political scandals like the Dreyfus Affair, plots to overthrow long-petrified regimes—all these pointed to a society divided against itself: Christian against Jew, rich against poor, free-thinker against man of faith, old against young, soldier against civilian. Gauguin, dying in 1903, just missed witnessing in every department of life what he had demanded only for art—"a breaking of all the old windows, even if we cut our fingers on the glass."

For many young artists this escape from the past was not easy, and nowhere was this truer than in Germany, where the military machine was already tuning up for murder. German officialdom felt, quite rightly, that an art based on a questioning attitude could prove inconvenient in other spheres as well, and the government did its best to suppress artistic independence. The director of the National Gallery in Berlin was dismissed, for instance, for buying too many modern French paintings. Under such conditions, free expression meant violent expression, and the free man was by definition a hunted man—a position that most German painters were quite incapable of dealing with.

Painting ranked high in German national life, but it was painting of a kind that depended on anecdote. Germans liked pictures of well-kept

In 1895, two years after painting *The Cry*, the dour Norwegian artist Edvard Munch made a linear interpretation of the picture in the lithograph above. In this black-and-white version, the scream seems to ring across the sky in ripples of schematic sound. Intensely concerned with social problems, with the alienation of the individual and with the anxieties of modern life, Munch and other northern European painters revealed their feelings in a style known as Expressionism.

fishermen mending their nets, of soldiers relaxing with nursemaids over a glass of beer, of preparations for a first communion, of lambs in springtime in the Tyrol. For deeper fare, to satisfy what the German art historian Wilhelm Worringer referred to as "the heavily oppressed inner life of northern humanity," Germans turned to poetry and novels, to the theater and the opera house. Painting was society's accomplice, and society did not let painters forget it. What this attitude produced was a kind of art described in 1900 by a very idealistic young man, Ernst Ludwig Kirchner, after a visit to a Munich art exhibit. "The paintings were as depressing as the public's indifference," wrote Kirchner. "Outside there was the flood of life, all color, all sunshine, all gladness. Inside, these pale, lifeless daubs. Why don't the worthy gentlemen paint real life?"

Five years later Kirchner and three of his friends decided to do something about it. Kirchner was then an architectural student in Dresden, and of the four crusaders—the others were Erich Heckel, Karl Schmidt-Rottluff and Fritz Bleyl—he was the only one with any formal art education. Nevertheless, banding together as *Die Brücke*, "the bridge," the four men set out to redeem German art. Dresden at the time was one of the most beautiful cities in the world, with a very lively cultural life. But it was a culture in which there was no place for disquiet. Kirchner and his friends were not so much rejected as ignored. They worked in empty shops on out-of-the-way streets, using their friends as models and relying on a handful of sympathizers for support. They took their inspiration partly from Van Gogh, whose work they had seen at a Dresden exhibit in 1905, and partly from primitive African and Polynesian art, of which there were some superb examples in the local ethnographic museum. Disdaining all ties with the conventional art world, they held their first exhibit in the showroom of a suburban lamp factory.

The Brücke believed not only in a new art, but in a new society. It stood for candor and truth in personal relationships, for the straightforward portrayal of social reality, for absolute faith in young people as against their titled and bemedalled elders. "We don't want art for art's sake," wrote one of its spokesmen, Iwan Goll. "We want art for people's sake." Using the same palette of pure unmixed colors that Matisse used, they achieved a completely different result. Where Matisse aimed for a sense of relaxed well-being, Kirchner and his friends were out to shock and provoke. Their candid portraits show people in awkward, half-dressed poses—pulling at a garter, sprawled across a bed—that make the viewer feel like an intruder. Their groups of nudes in the open air are identifiable people undressed in public and are suggestive of acts even more abhorrent to public order. Unlike Gauguin's naked South Sea islanders, who belong to a distant and doomed culture, the Brücke nudes are ordinary Germans taking off their clothes in conservative Saxony.

In this act of social sabotage, color was once more the great henchman: the Brücke's colors were high and strong, as aggressive as their subject matter. "May God protect us! Bad times are on the way!" Edvard Munch is said to have exclaimed when he first saw a collection of their lithographs. Kirchner, painting one of his lady friends lying on her stomach, her backside as blue as a baboon's, might well have been echoing one of the Brücke's favorite authors, Friedrich Nietzsche. "Anyone who wishes to be creative," wrote Nietzsche, "must first blast and destroy all social values."

Yet strong color is not in itself subversive. Delacroix had observed in his diary that the ideas commonly generated by yellow, orange and red were "joy and plenty." And in spite of 19th Century Europe's general preference for brownish, spinachy-green narrative paintings, there were still people whose color sense operated in a much higher key. In Russia, above all, Western ideas of nuance and subtlety simply did not apply. A five-minute walk through the Kremlin reveals on every hand a color sense that is direct and full-hearted. The buildings of the Kremlin are alive with color, inside and out, and that color is used with extraordinary freedom and assurance. Sooner or later Russian painters, conscientiously imitating the subdued palette of bygone French and Italian painting, were bound to realize that their strength lay in this ancestral attitude toward color.

The Russian who got the point soonest was Wassily Kandinsky, a painter who had embarked on his painting career at an even later point in his life than Matisse. Until well into adult life Kandinsky, too, had meant to be a lawyer. Not until 1896, when he was offered a law professorship in a provincial university, did he finally realize that painting was his true profession. Turning down the academic post, Kandinsky went off to Munich to study art. Despite this change in careers, Kandinsky looked and acted all his life like a member of the learned professions. He was precise and sober in his dress and kept his studio as clean and neat as an operating room. He was widely read and could talk with authority on many subjects—music, anthropology, the natural sciences, comparative religion, literature in several languages and the theater.

As early as 1889, on a trip to the provinces to collect information on Russian peasant law, Kandinsky had been struck by the intensity of the peasants' untutored color sense. All around him he saw houses, clothes, furniture and furnishings so richly ornamented that everything seemed to dissolve in color. When he himself began to paint, he drew upon this ancestral tradition. One of his early paintings, a scene evocative of medieval Russia, *The Motley Life (page 67)*, is an attempt to use color with the same vigor and freedom and purity that he had found in folk art. He also assigned certain meanings to colors—much as Old Russia liked to refer to the "raspberry note" of the small bells worn by horses. Red, for instance, in Kandinsky's mind stood for "purposeful power," yellow for uncontrollable aggression and "absolute green" was supremely restful. White was a symbol of silence—the silence of emptiness awaiting fulfillment; black was also a symbol of silence—but of another and more final sort.

Unlike the Brücke, which fought its battles at home and largely in isolation, surrounded by a hostile society, Kandinsky traveled widely and was a true cosmopolitan. He was as much at home in Paris and Mu-

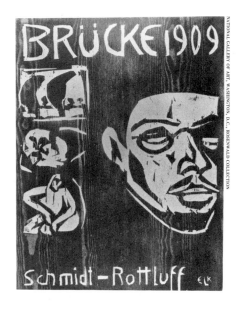

Ernst Ludwig Kirchner, a founder of the Dresden artists' group *Die Brücke* (The Bridge), made this woodcut in 1909 for the cover of a portfolio containing lithographs and an etching by Karl Schmidt-Rottluff, another founding member. In 1906, a year after the group was formed, Schmidt-Rottluff stated their aim: "To attract all revolutionary and fermenting elements, that is the purpose implied in the name 'Brücke.'"

nich as he was in his native Russia, and he knew what was going on everywhere in the world of art. What set him apart from other painters was his entirely original color sense, and eventually this color sense moved with him into abstract art. Kandinsky, around 1908, discovered quite by accident that color could work independently of the object with which it was associated. Returning one evening to his home in Munich, Kandinsky came face to face in his studio with a painting he had recently completed. For a moment its colors, in the twilight, spoke to him so strongly in themselves and for themselves that the subject matter of the picture did not matter—and the impact of the picture was, if anything, all the stronger for it. From this he inferred that it might be possible to dispense with subject matter entirely, and that the result might be all gain and no loss.

But it took him several years to work this out. Kandinsky had previously used color in a straightforward, descriptive way, to heighten the emotional content of a particular scene—to evoke, for instance, the pageantry of the Middle Ages or the blazing sun of North Africa. Now he began to use color to express his own states of mind. Instead of choosing the contents of his pictures, he stood aside and allowed those contents to choose him, deliberately opening himself to imagery brought in from the unconscious. The result was a combination of forms and colors that were meant to act upon the observer in a logical, predictable way—since each form and color had for Kandinsky a very specific meaning.

Pure abstract painting was born in Germany in 1910 with this completely nonobjective watercolor by the Russian-born Wassily Kandinsky. True to his theory that art should provide direct communication between painter and viewer, with no preconceived language of imagery to encumber the artist's spontaneous freedom, Kandinsky left this epoch-making watercolor untitled.

If those forms and colors sometimes reflected the real world as well as Kandinsky's own unconscious, this was a fact he neither stressed nor ignored. The cannons that crept into *Improvisation 30—Cannon* could be explained, he said, "by the continual talk of war that has been going on." Kandinsky was no fool about world affairs despite a strong element of mysticism in his make-up, and like every other intelligent European he saw disaster coming. The cannons, the churches blasting off like rockets, the fragments of landscape lying about, were all expressive of a world in dissolution. Yet the painting itself, as a composition, is absolutely firm. "Make sure the corners are heavy," Kandinsky told himself as he painted it, and indeed the corners are pinned down as firmly as those of a big circus tent. Above all, the colors work together to create a sense of absolute stability. Through color, the painting speaks of another world, one that lies beyond the petty concerns of men —one that will outlast them.

Kandinsky believed that it was the artist's role "to speak of mystery in terms of mystery," and to help "suffering, searching, tormented souls" discover their common bond with animate and inanimate nature. This was a far cry from the social realism of the Brücke. It was even further removed from Matisse's artistic concerns. To Matisse, Kandinsky's credo must have seemed pure dementia—but neither can he have had much sympathy for the Brücke's wish to change society. Yet curiously it was to Matisse that both Kandinsky and the Brücke often looked for leadership.

His attraction was not his reputation for wildness. Indeed Kandinsky and the Brücke must have known, as most painters did on even the slightest acquaintance with Matisse, that the label "wild beast" was ill-deserved. Rather, they were drawn to this entirely rational man by his calculated use of color, a color more intense, more ingenious and less dependent upon everyday experience than anything painters had hitherto been able to manage. Matisse in effect had brought electricity to a civilization based on candles.

For Matisse, however, this great service to art was no more than a passing phase, immensely invigorating but limited. Fauve painting was a sprinter's painting, and Matisse was a long-distance runner. He spoke later and without regret of his Fauve period as a time "when the noting down of my immediate and superficial color sensations was enough for me." Fauve color belonged to a certain moment and that moment could not be prolonged.

The Salon d'Automne of 1905 had scarcely closed its doors when Matisse began work on a very large canvas in which Fauvism is only part of the magic. *Joy of Life (study on page 82)* is one of the great paintings of the 20th Century. It looks both forward and backward, and says things about art and the hidden energies of life as well as about Matisse and the future course of his career. It is a picture that derives directly from Matisse's summer in Collioure, but it also has to do with ideas that had haunted the European imagination for centuries—ideas relating to the age-old dream of a secret garden free from guilt and worldly care.

Matisse took enormous trouble with the painting. First he sketched a remembered clearing in the woods near Collioure, which had a distant view of the sea. Then he did a great many drawings of a naked model in the open air, remembering the look of Collioure fishermen dancing on the shore, but also remembering the way Greek vase-painters treated the human figure. For his reclining figures, he turned to his memory of Seurat's languorous Parisians in *Sunday Afternoon on the Island of La Grande Jatte.* And when he tackled the problem of composing these elements into a coherent whole, he remembered the bacchanals of a long succession of European painters, running from Bellini and Titian, through Rubens and Poussin, to Watteau and Ingres.

Yet most people, seeing the *Joy of Life* for the first time at the 1906 Salon des Indépendants, thought it willfully original—unlike any painting ever done before. Matisse had treated the trees as if they were a series of stage flats, and the carefree people in the scene—dancing, making love, playing the pipes—suggested the characters in a traditional classic ballet. But within the tradition, there were some very odd things. The serpentine woman twined with ivy at the extreme left looked more like an Art Nouveau lampstand than a human being; the couple making love in the foreground seemed to have, between them, only one head. Some of the people were impossibly large by the normal standards of perspective, and others were impossibly small.

Joy of Life initiated a lot of things, both for Matisse and for others. Its sinuous, sculptural poses became standard among sculptors of monumental figures, and its vigorous round dance was obviously the forerunner of Matisse's own famous *Dancers,* completed some four years later. In more general terms, *Joy of Life* declared Matisse's intention of being accepted as a painter on his own terms and on no one else's. Having examined most of the great art of the past, he knew that many of its themes were worth keeping, but he also knew that they could not be treated in the same way. Similarly, he knew that Fauve color, for all its striking effects, did not allow him to say the complex things he wanted to say. *Joy of Life* is a masterpiece of lyrical color, but it is not color used to intensify action—it *is* the action. The dancing figures, the lovers locked in emblematic embrace, the musicians playing on their pipes are no more alive than statues. It is the color that transports the viewer into another world.

Matisse set such great store by *Joy of Life* that it was his only entry in the 1906 Salon des Indépendants, but the audience, far from sharing his enthusiasm for it, was dumbfounded. The painting was clearly the result of long and patient labor, but what did it mean? Its subject was clearly erotic, but it did not seem to aim at sexual provocation. Nor did it seem at all to be a criticism of life or society, though it did hint an oblique criticism of other painters who attempted such subjects. It was in its way profoundly polemical—Matisse's own arguments for what he thought painting should be—and like all good polemics, it enraged a lot of people. One of the people most enraged was Matisse's old friend Signac, who announced to one of his disciples that Matisse had "gone completely to the dogs. He's taken a canvas eight feet long, surrounded some odd characters with a line as thick as your thumb and covered the whole thing with flat, well-defined color areas, which, pure as they are, disgust me."

Fortunately there was one person who understood what Matisse was up to. The poet Guillaume Apollinaire was Matisse's exact opposite—impulsive where Matisse was measured and cautious, extravagantly social where Matisse begrudged every moment spent away from the studio, adventurous where Matisse double-checked every new move. Apollinaire was one of the most irresistible personalities of the century. He also happened to love painting, and he wrote a great deal about it. What he wrote was not always well-founded (Braque once said that Apollinaire could not tell Rembrandt from Rubens), but people read him simply because he was Apollinaire. Also, he moved among painters as an artist among artists, and so they spoke to him freely and in full confidence. Consequently, his articles were often a very good guide to how painters really felt.

Apollinaire often talked with Matisse—Matisse's children still remember his roly-poly presence in their home and his insatiable appetite for preserved ginger—and he defended Matisse when most of the art world was anxious to look the other way. Critics complained, he wrote, that *Fauve* was "too mild for Matisse, that *Fauvissime*, 'wildest of wild beasts,' would be better," but the truth was that "if Matisse is an innovator, as he certainly is, he renovates more than he innovates." Then he would go on to woo his readers toward Matisse with references to the painter's solid family life, to the quality of the food served by Madame Matisse ("the family table, without being lavish, is delicious"), to the excellence of Matisse's liqueurs, brought back from Collioure.

Apollinaire was the first to say in print that Matisse's art was above all an art of equilibrium, in which instinct and acquired knowledge were made to work together. Questioned about this, Matisse told Apollinaire that the artist had to find his own inmost personality and rely upon it entirely, and that this could not be done through introspection alone. He had to pit himself against the giants of the past, confront them directly. "If the fight is mortal," he said, "and the personality of the artist collapses, then that's the way it has to be." Apollinaire was also the first to report in print the full extent of Matisse's interest in other forms of art: "the hieratic art of the Egyptians, the refined Greek art, the voluptuous Cambodians, the work of the ancient Peruvians and the African tribal statues, proportioned according to the passions that provoked them."

Through Apollinaire, people became genuinely interested in Matisse's ideas, and in 1908 the magazine *La Grande Revue* invited him to speak for himself. The article, "A Painter's Notes," became an immediate sensation and was translated almost at once into German and Russian. At a moment when Expressionism was rampant and violence was visible everywhere in art, Matisse disposed of Expressionist ideas in a line or two. "To my mind," he wrote, "expression is not a matter of passion mirrored on the human face or revealed by a violent gesture. When I paint a picture, its every detail is expressive. The place occupied by figures or objects, the empty spaces around them, the proportions, everything plays a part." He was equally short with the Impressionists, whose work was still a living issue for the public. "A rapid rendering of a landscape," he wrote, "represents only one moment of its appearance. I . . . prefer to discover its more enduring character and content, even at the risk of sacrificing some of its more pleasing qualities." As for the color theories of Signac and his friends, these too were shown the door: "When I choose a color it is not because of any scientific theory. It comes from observation, from feeling, from the innermost nature of the experience in question."

Matisse was against violent expression, against the rendering of fugitive impressions, against all forms of pseudoscientific doctrine. He wanted a considered art, an art of serenity from which everything nonessential had been pared away, an art of which he himself was to be the master. "I cannot copy nature like a servant. I interpret nature, and nature must submit herself to the spirit of the picture." He was a conservative, then, rejecting the painting styles of the moment. But he was also in the truest sense a revolutionary. For mere imitators of the past he had nothing but disdain. "We belong to our time," he wrote. "We share its opinions, its preferences and its delusions. All artists bear the mark of their time, and the great artists are the ones in whom that mark lies deepest." And Matisse knew, though he did not say, that the great artist is the one who takes the whole burden of his time upon himself, who paints not for color's sake, or for heaven's sake, or for pity's sake, but for his own sake. Matisse accepted that burden, and lived with it and proved himself right.

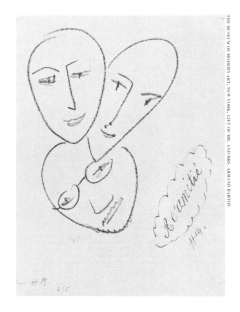

This 1950 lithograph, *Apollinaire, Rouveyre, Matisse,* is Matisse's tribute to two of his early admirers and friends. The poet-critic Guillaume Apollinaire *(top, left),* the first public champion of Matisse's work, had died, weakened by war wounds, in the 1918 flu epidemic. André Rouveyre, a writer and caricaturist who shared the artist's love of the south of France, still lived in Vence, near Matisse, when the lithograph was made. Matisse inscribed the triple portrait "To friendship" in a curlycued border, like an entry in a 19th Century album of mementos.

The "Wild Beasts"

The pictures are a riot of color; the sky is cream, the shadows green, the tree trunks red. Even today, after more than 60 years, the viewer is jolted by the power of their colors and is disturbingly pleased by their effect. When such paintings were exhibited at the Salon d'Automne in 1905, Parisians too were shocked—but not with pleasure. So aggressively irrational did the paintings seem that the painters who had made them were nicknamed *fauves*, or "wild beasts." Ironically, the leader of the "wild beasts" was the sober Matisse.

Why did Matisse, who was such a careful observer, deliberately ignore the colors of nature for these aberrant hues? To Matisse and the Fauves color served to transmit the artist's intense feeling for his subject; color stood for the emotion of the artist as he went about his work.

Matisse's pictures were shown very early in Germany, where painters were already trying techniques that would jog traditional German art out of its representational rut. In Dresden and Munich particularly, daring young men used bold, abstract color to express themselves and thus earned their name, "Expressionists."

Both the Expressionists of Germany and the Fauves of France were indebted to Van Gogh, Gauguin and Cézanne; both movements at their most intense were short lived, burning out quickly like bursts from a Roman candle. But Matisse remained a Fauve in principle for the rest of his days—color conveyed his emotion.

This light and lyrical scene is a typical Fauve painting by Matisse. The brushwork is quick, the colors audacious; the carefree gaiety of a summer day is unmistakable. Charming as this painting seems today, it was attacked in 1905 with the other Fauve paintings by one critic as "the barbaric and naïve sport of a child who plays with the box of colors he just got as a Christmas present."

The Open Window, 1905

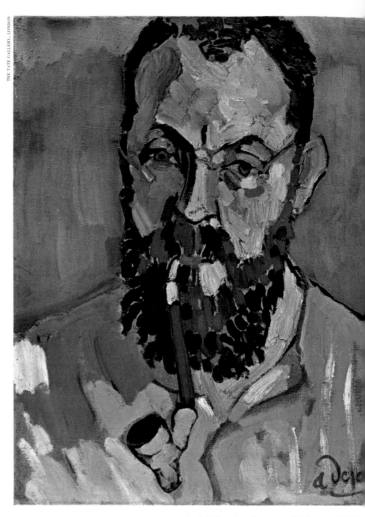

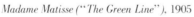

Madame Matisse ("The Green Line"), 1905   André Derain: *Portrait of Matisse*, 1905

The first time the three leading Fauves—Matisse, André Derain and Maurice de Vlaminck—got together was at a Van Gogh exhibition in 1901. Van Gogh was an inspiration to all three. "I use color in a completely arbitrary way in order to express myself powerfully," the Dutchman had written to his brother some 15 years before. Van Gogh had been dead almost a dozen years, but the Fauves, through their work, proved to be kindred spirits.

Matisse and Derain had been acquainted for a couple of years; both were serious students of art who were working toward Fauvism through study and experimentation. Derain's friend, Vlaminck, was the opposite: a wildly impulsive artist who made his paintings glow like red-hot coals. Matisse described his meeting with Vlaminck at the Van Gogh show in this way: "I saw Derain in the company of an enormous young fellow who proclaimed his enthusiasm in a voice of authority. . . .I still think Derain was a bit afraid of him. But he admired him for his enthusiasm and his passion."

Whatever their personality differences, the three

Maurice de Vlaminck: *Portrait of Derain*, 1905

André Derain: *Portrait of Vlaminck*, 1905

arrived at Fauvism almost simultaneously, but individually. Vlaminck's style was crude, as is seen in his portrait of Derain *(above, left)*. The paints are thick on the canvas, laid on in heavy smears; the eyelids are weighty, the mustache wanders off the face, the skin tone and background in one section are nearly identical. Derain's portrait of Vlaminck *(above, right)* shows a lighter, more delicate touch. The colors are softer than Vlaminck's, the brushstrokes finer; the ambiance, from the cocked bowler hat to the cheery yellow background,

is more sophisticated. Derain's fine sensitivities are also manifest in his portrait of Matisse *(opposite)*.

Of all the Fauves, however, Matisse had the surest hand, as is seen by his portrait of his wife *(opposite)*, nicknamed "The Green Line" by the Michael Steins, who first owned it. The green splits the face in relief and saves it from being lost in the forceful background. Here Matisse has used one of his favorite devices: he made the background so strong that the subject must emerge on its own. The result is a study of imposed harmony.

André Derain: *View of Collioure*, 1905

Vlaminck and Derain, although of vastly different temperaments, fitted the popular notion of the artist as a rather disreputable bohemian. They worked together briefly in what had been a decrepit old restaurant in Chatou, a suburb of Paris. They consorted with bums, beggars and prostitutes, and they took a vain pride in their physical strength, frequently interrupting work for strenuous bike rides and rowing races. "We were not real bohemians," Vlaminck said, referring to himself and

Derain. "Just nonconformists. We didn't belong."

Derain's work suffered from his excessively intellectual bent. He became increasingly conservative, often trying to match himself against the masters and—in his mind— failing. "The greatest danger in art is too much knowledge," he said. But at his best, his touch was true, guided by a sure sense of light, movement and beauty. When he worked with Matisse at Collioure in 1905 (*above*), his work reflected their shared belief that painting

Maurice de Vlaminck: *Landscape with Red Trees*, 1906

should always be pleasing to the eye.

Unlike Derain, Vlaminck never compared his talent with past masters. He was a blatant self-promoter who took keen pleasure in giving art history broad swipes with the back of his hand. "Visiting museums bastardizes the personality, just as hobnobbing with priests makes you lose your faith," he once said. Striking out at his canvases, he worked in furious bursts, often spreading the oil paint on directly from the tubes, as had Van Gogh. His talents were many-sided. A pugnacious giant, Vlaminck was an accomplished musician and writer. And he was also an anarchist who worked off his hatred of the social establishment through his art. "Painting was an abscess which drained off the evil in me," he said. "What I could have achieved in social context by throwing a bomb. . .I have tried to express in art. . . . Thus I have been able to use my destructive instincts in order to re-create a sensitive, living and free world."

While the Fauves set Paris in an uproar, the Expressionists were trying to inflame not only the German art world, but their entire repressive, rigid society. One school, Die Brücke, or "The Bridge" (to the future), established a studio in a former butcher's shop in Dresden, where work and talk went on all night, and models and artists enjoyed a communal life. The two paintings on this page by Kirchner and Heckel show this passion for freedom and spontaneity. Another school of Expressionists was formed in Munich as Der Blaue Reiter (The Blue Rider), a name coined by two of its leaders, Wassily Kandinsky and Franz Marc. Kandinsky, a Russian expatriate and former professor, often painted fond memories of his homeland, using color to convey his spiritual longing *(opposite page)*. Similarly, the German Marc used color, shape and rhythm to dramatize the integration of all creatures in nature.

Ernst Ludwig Kirchner: *Blue Nude with Straw Hat*, 1908

Erich Heckel: *At the Pond in the Wood*, 1910

66

Wassily Kandinsky: *The Motley Life*, 1907

Franz Marc: *The Yellow Cow*, 1911

67

IV

An Audience from Abroad

Matisse in his late 30s was not rich in the way that young painters are often rich today, but there was a moment when it was clear that with reasonable luck he would never be poor again. The moment came sometime between March 1906 and February 1907. On the former date the art dealer Théodore Druet offered him a one-man show, to which Matisse sent 55 pictures—all but a few of which came straight back to his studio when the show closed. On the latter date a new young art dealer, D.-H. Kahnweiler, arrived in Paris from Germany and was quickly able to corral such painters as Derain, Vlaminck, Braque and Picasso. But Kahnweiler never approached Matisse because, he said, Matisse "was already too big for me." Somewhere along the line in the intervening 10 months, Matisse had changed from an unsalable firebrand to a man of substance. He had acquired what all painters dream of: a group of solid, serious, durable patrons.

With one exception all of these patrons were foreigners. The only Frenchman to see the point of Matisse was Marcel Sembat, the Socialist politician who represented Montmartre in the Chamber of Deputies. Sembat had begun to collect Matisse's paintings in the early days of Fauvism, and never lost his admiration for his work. In 1920 Sembat published the first monograph on Matisse, and in 1922 his generous bequest to the Grenoble Museum put it 20 years ahead of other French museums in the possession of Matisse paintings.

Among Matisse's foreign patrons, the honor of being first usually goes to Leo and Gertrude Stein, who bought *Woman with the Hat*—reputedly for around $100—from the Salon d'Automne and carried it off to the apartment they shared at 27 Rue de Fleurus. Matisse was impressed by their faith. French feeling against the picture ran so hot and strong at the time that he had forbidden Madame Matisse to go to the Salon, and Matisse himself went only once. But the Steins were not ordinary patrons. By French standards they were naïve, but they also had a fearless and articulate preference for the new. They were eager to learn but also innately self-confident.

Leo and Gertrude Stein were the children and grandchildren of Amer-

Matisse expressed the visual excitement he felt in Morocco with the warm colors of this still life painted during his second visit there. Lush and inviting, the fruit in the bowl is set off by a scattering of green leaves, while the flowered tablecloth and colorful background supply a touch of gaiety.

Oranges, 1912

69

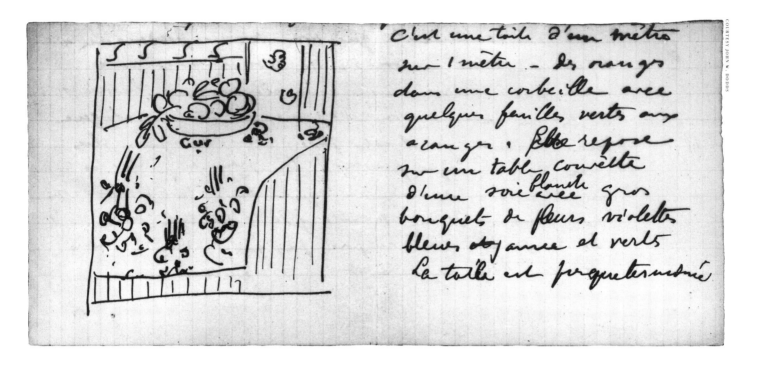

A sketch and color notes for the painting *Oranges* appear above on the fragment of a letter Matisse sent to Michael Stein in 1912. Apparently Matisse was not yet satisfied with the design and was trying out an idea on his friend. For the finished work *(see page 68 for comparison)*, he kept the fruit and flowered tablecloth essentially the same, but broke the original background elements into a greater variety of horizontal, vertical and oblique lines and colors, and replaced the stripes below the cloth with solid red and purple. Picasso bought the Matisse painting for his own collection during World War II.

ica's robust, mid-19th Century expansionism. Sensitive they might be, but in the last analysis they thought their judgment as good as anyone else's. They had money—not a lot, but enough—from family-owned clothing stores in Baltimore and Pittsburgh, and from holdings in the Omnibus Cable Company of San Francisco and the Central Pacific Railroad. In Baltimore they had made their mark as cultivated people, but they also knew how to work. Gertrude had been a serious student of medicine at Johns Hopkins at a time when only a rare woman dared to enter the field, and had missed out on her diploma only because she refused to make up a flunked course given by a professor who bored her. Leo cared enough about art to spend every vacation from Harvard touring the world's great museums, and for a time was collecting material for a life of Mantegna, a project he abandoned only when he realized that he preferred esthetics to history. After Harvard, Leo became a disciple of Bernard Berenson, and was often at Berenson's Florentine villa, I Tatti—although Berenson sometimes found Leo's earnest scholarship tiresome (Leo, he once said, "was always inventing the umbrella").

As children, the Steins had been inseparable—Leo once referred to their attraction for each other as "the family romance." In Paris they soon became the center of the bohemian art world. Even in that world they were a funny pair. Leo, with his unceasing flow of talk, his presumed wealth, his bald head and superabundant beard, his corduroy pants and "bacchic" sandals, struck the French as a mysterious, contradictory figure. Gertrude was even odder: a squat, thick-set, pear-shaped young woman with a monumental head and a capacity for saying things that mattered in a very few words. At the time, however, no one took the future author of some immensely influential poetry and prose to be a near-genius. It was Leo who set the intellectual pace. Among his friends, who were many, and his amours, who were hardly less numerous, Leo was known as a man who would achieve great things—if only he could make up his mind what he wanted to do.

Leo's letters reveal him as vain, touchy and self-important. Nevertheless he was briefly, according to art historian Alfred Barr, perhaps the world's most discerning collector of 20th Century art. Between 1905, when he and Gertrude bought *Woman with the Hat*, and 1909, when he tired of the game, Leo put together a superb collection of modern painting. Berthe Weill knew him well—Leo referred to her as "the funny little squinting near-sighted old lady who sympathized with revolutionaries, good, bad and indifferent"—and it was through Berthe Weill that he came to buy *Woman with the Hat*. Berthe Weill told him of Matisse's chagrin over the picture's reception. "Matisse had thought that this time he had played the ace of trumps," Leo wrote, "and apparently it would take nothing." He and Gertrude went to look at the picture in the Salon, got over its strangeness and decided to buy it. "It was what I had unknowingly been waiting for," he wrote.

Having bought the painting, they soon arranged to meet the artist, and Leo, who knew an intellectual when he saw one, was delighted. Matisse's mind was like the well-stocked, well-ordered minds of the people with whom the Steins had associated in Baltimore. "Matisse was really intelligent," he noted. "He was also witty, and capable of saying exactly what he meant about art." At a time when most Frenchmen thought of Matisse as someone who just splashed paint around, Leo Stein got the point of Matisse's working methods: "He is intuitive, he is intelligent, in his way he is as persistent as Cézanne himself; and his best compositions are full, complete, veritable pictorial finalities such as one rarely finds." Before long Matisse paintings were hanging one on top of another at 27 Rue de Fleurus. The Steins bought freely, out of genuine passion, and in bulk: *Woman with the Hat* in 1905, *Joy of Life* in 1906, *Blue Nude* in 1907.

Matisse was glad to have such firm support, but he was not bowled

Paintings by Cézanne, Matisse, Renoir and Picasso jammed the walls of Gertrude Stein's salon on the Rue de Fleurus. Here Miss Stein (*right*) and her life-long companion Alice B. Toklas, often seated in this fireplace corner of the room, held court for favored artists. It was here, in fact, that Gertrude once gave a luncheon for all the living painters whose work she owned, taking delight in seating each man opposite his own picture. No one noticed the arrangement except the alert Matisse, who was annoyed rather than pleased. According to Miss Stein, he later upbraided her laughingly, saying, "Mademoiselle Gertrude, the world is a theater for you, but there are theaters and theaters, and when you listen so carefully to me and so attentively and do not hear a word I say then I do say you are very wicked." Most likely Matisse was put out because Picasso was replacing him in Miss Stein's favor.

over by it. Leo himself once observed that "Matisse has always been a very good businessman, and why not? We did not buy his paintings because of his beautiful eyes, but because we were interested in what he was doing. . . ." Perhaps Matisse sensed that the interest would fade, that Leo was by nature giddy and unfocused and that Gertrude, although vastly more stable, had no real feeling for art. In any case it is certain that the person he liked best in the Stein family was Mrs. Michael Stein, the wife of their older brother. It was primarily thanks to Michael Stein's skill as an investor that Leo and Gertrude did not have to bother about money. And it was Michael's wife Sarah who very soon became Matisse's most staunch and loyal admirer.

The charcoal sketch above is a study by Matisse for his portrait of Michael Stein's wife, Sarah *(page 82)*, the artist's favorite of all the Stein family. Sarah was responsible for the first sale of a Matisse to an art collector in America. She bought *Nude in a Wood* for a New York friend George Of, who had seen the Matisse pictures she had brought with her on a quick trip home in 1906. Impressed by these works, the first Matisses to come to the United States, Of asked Sarah to buy a Matisse for him sight unseen; she fulfilled the commission on her return to France.

The Michael Steins lived on Rue Madame in a modest apartment that had none of the panache of the bohemian establishment on Rue de Fleurus. But though Matisse was always made much of when he visited Leo and Gertrude, he was a great deal happier at the Michael Steins. Sarah Stein was an impulsive, affectionate young woman who had once studied painting, and Matisse thought her a person of exceptional finesse and discernment: "Mrs. Michael Stein," he wrote many years later, "was the really intelligently sensitive member of the family." Also, after the self-important posturing that was *de rigueur* on Rue de Fleurus, he found Sarah's unspoiled girlish ways a pleasant contrast. He got into the habit of going regularly to Rue Madame to talk with Sarah and her husband, feeling that with them he could speak freely, without danger of having his confidences bruited all over town.

The fullest and funniest but not the most reliable account of this period in Matisse's life is to be found in Gertrude Stein's light-hearted book, *The Autobiography of Alice B. Toklas*—ostensibly the memoir of the wispy young woman who joined Gertrude in 1907, to become her lifelong companion. Written long after the events it describes (it was published in 1933), the *Autobiography* contains errors of fact, taste and affection. Leo Stein called it "a rather clever superstructure on a basis of impenetrable stupidity." Georges Braque was more blunt. "Miss Stein," he wrote, "understood nothing of what went on around her. . . . She never went beyond the stage of the tourist." Matisse said for publication that much of the book was sheer invention, "more like a harlequin's costume . . . sewn together without taste and without relation to reality." In private he went much further; Gertrude Stein, he said, was a "king-sized blockhead."

The book's references to Matisse are indeed often disparaging. At one point, speaking of her cook, Hélène, Miss Stein wrote, "Hélène had her opinions; she did not for instance like Matisse. She said a Frenchman should not stay unexpectedly to a meal particularly if he asked the servant beforehand what there was for dinner. She said that foreigners had a perfect right to do these things but not a Frenchman. . . . So when Miss Stein said to her, Monsieur Matisse is staying for dinner this evening, she would say, in that case I will not make an omelet but fry the eggs. It takes the same number of eggs and the same amount of butter but it shows less respect, and he will understand."

No one likes to be made fun of in print, and Frenchmen are especially incensed by the jibes of foreigners: the privilege of entering French life is not one that is expected to be abused. But there is a further possible reason for Matisse's annoyance with *The Autobiography of Alice B. Toklas.* Gertrude Stein makes it quite clear that in her view the one painter worth bothering about in the Paris of her youth was a young Spaniard just starting to make his way: Pablo Picasso.

Matisse and Picasso met at the Steins in the fall of 1906. Fernande Olivier, Picasso's companion at the time, says in her memoirs that at this meeting "Matisse was very much master of himself. Picasso was always rather sullen and restrained at such times, and it was Matisse who shone." Matisse had reason to feel superior. His most important painting, *Joy of Life,* dominated the Steins' drawing room and he was, after all, Picasso's senior by 12 years; Picasso was then only 25. But it was a misleading beginning. Picasso had known Leo and Gertrude Stein for almost a year, and had already completed his monumental portrait of Gertrude—for which she sat more than 80 times. During those sittings she and Picasso had achieved a genuine rapport, quite different from her relationship with Matisse. Picasso was mercurial, inquisitive, opportunistic, quite evidently a man of genius; Matisse, with his intrinsic reserve and his measured way of speaking, was not. Gertrude Stein was not profoundly committed to painting as painting, but she was committed to exceptional human beings. And she recognized, from the very start, that Picasso was at the very top of that class.

The fact that Matisse and Picasso had not met before is less extraordinary than it might seem. Picasso lived and worked in Montmartre and seldom came down its hills to Paris proper; Matisse never went up to Montmartre. Neither man went out for the sake of going out, but a patron, especially a foreign patron, had certain claims on a painter. Gertrude Stein had no particular trouble getting Matisse and Picasso into her house at the same time, but it is doubtful that any other hostess could have done it with such ease thereafter. Matisse and Picasso were never rivals in the commonplace sense, but neither were they close friends. Each recognized the other as a supreme professional. Pi-

In 1911 Matisse was anxious about *The Painter's Family (page 87),* his work in progress when he sent the postcard above to Michael Stein in San Francisco. "It is well under way," he wrote in the note, above a sketch of the painting, ". . . but I am uncertain of its success." Genuinely fond of Michael Stein and his wife, Matisse did portraits of them both in Paris in 1916 *(page 82).* The photograph at left shows Matisse at work on Michael's larger than life-size, austere portrait. More conventional than most of Matisse's portraits of the time, the picture perhaps reflects the deep personal esteem the painter had for his subject.

Miss Etta Cone *(above)* and her sister, Dr. Claribel Cone *(below)*, were perceptive collectors of 43 Matisse paintings. Women of great learning and outstanding individuality, they also had their eccentric side. Dr. Claribel was said to be so insistent on her comfort and privacy that, when World War I broke out while she was visiting Germany, she chose to remain there through the war-torn years rather than risk having to share crowded accommodations during the return home. The fastidious Miss Etta once typed a complete Gertrude Stein manuscript letter by letter since, having failed to ask permission to read the book, she did not feel that it was fitting to take notice of the words.

casso once spoke of Matisse and himself as the "North Pole and South Pole" of art—meaning no doubt that in temperament they could not have been further apart, but also meaning that they functioned as landmarks, without which the map of modern art did not make sense.

At the time of their first meeting there was no direct parallel between their activities. Picasso was just emerging from his Blue and Rose Period canvases—delicious, romantic visions that stayed within the bounds of everyday experience. Soon he would begin to develop Cubism, a kind of painting that seemed to many people more radical and more promising than anything Matisse had put forward. The color revolution pioneered by Matisse was a revolution of feeling; it empowered painters to express themselves with a new directness and candor. The Cubism pioneered by Picasso was a revolution in construction. While Matisse moved toward a two-dimensional art conceived in flat areas of pure color, Picasso was giving the world a new idea of the third dimension. The two were going in completely opposite directions. Yet it would have been unnatural for Picasso not to wish to overtake Matisse as an artist, and equally unnatural for Matisse not to regard this with something more than mere curiosity.

Shortly after meeting Matisse, Picasso set about painting what is probably the most famous picture of this century, *Les Demoiselles d'Avignon*, a canvas dominated by five massive female nudes with masklike faces and angular bodies. The origins of this painting are immensely complex, but unquestionably Matisse was, in one way or another, on Picasso's mind from time to time when he did it. With his genius for fastening upon things that could be of use to him, Picasso had recently fastened on African art. Just how this came about is still a matter of controversy. Matisse, however, had been collecting African sculpture for some time, and no doubt had shown his collection to Picasso when Picasso came to call on him at his apartment. Picasso also had before him during this period the example of Matisse's *Joy of Life*, which hung in 27 Rue de Fleurus, a painting in which Matisse had masterfully summed up all his preoccupations to date. It cannot be pure coincidence that almost immediately Picasso began to paint a comparably ambitious picture. Finally, there is a direct relation between the seated figure in Picasso's painting and a seated figure in Cézanne's *Bathers*, a painting then owned by Matisse.

After the appearance of *Les Demoiselles d'Avignon*, a well-judged wariness marked the two painters' personal relations, even though they continued to see each other socially. There was a period, for instance, when Matisse took Picasso riding with him, and, wittingly or not, set a pace that invariably left the nonriding Picasso stiff and sore. And much has been made of the fact that when they exchanged paintings, neither gave the other his best work. Nevertheless, after the end of World War II, when the two were more or less neighbors in the south of France, they drew closer together. Matisse presented Picasso with the dove that served as model for his famous peace poster, and with the striped Melanesian idol that confronted visitors to Picasso's villa in the late 1950s. Picasso, who values few persons' opinions, often invited Matisse to look at his work—and when Matisse became too ill to leave home, Picasso hired a truck and took his paintings to Matisse so that the aged master could examine them at his leisure. Not long after Matisse died, a friend remarked to Picasso on what seemed to him the influence of Matisse in one of his new canvases. "Ah yes," said Picasso, "you see I have to paint for both of us now."

The personal magnetism that so quickly attracted collectors to Picasso was absent in Matisse. Every new enthusiast for Matisse's work was a precious possession, and the year 1906 was memorable for his acquisition of two such patrons, the strong-minded American maiden ladies, Dr. Claribel and Miss Etta Cone. The Cones had been friends of the Steins since Baltimore days, and like them were genuine cosmopolitans. They too had a comfortable private income—in their case, from cotton mills founded by their brothers with money borrowed from their father, a first-generation German-Jewish immigrant.

Dr. Claribel Cone, even more drawn to medicine than Gertrude Stein, was one of the first woman doctors in America. Just a few inches over five feet high, with large hands and feet and a marked tendency to spread out below the waist, she cut an even stranger figure than her friend. Paradoxically, however, Dr. Claribel had a great sense of style. She invariably wore black, but she fancied theatrical accessories, often putting them together in combinations that stopped just short of the ridiculous. At the opera she would appear with silver skewers from India in her hair, massive Renaissance jewelry upon her bosom, mountains of shawls from Spain and the Orient draped over her shoulders. Dr. Claribel had a lot to say, most of it worth hearing, and a voice that compelled attention. Miss Etta, her sister, was equally firm in her opinions, although as a person she was gentle and withdrawn and much less extravagant in her costume. Their qualities as art collectors are manifested in the Cone Collection of the Baltimore Museum, but their qualities as human beings were just as remarkable: as patrons, the Cones were constant, honorable and open-minded.

Matisse met the Cones in January 1906, when they were taken to call on him by Mrs. Michael Stein. They bought at once, for $20, a drawing and a watercolor, and they went on buying for 30 years. Unlike Leo and Gertrude Stein, who later unloaded their Matisses, the Cones held onto theirs. And unlike other Matisse collectors, who dropped out when his prices rose, they continued to bid for his work on the open market. When *Blue Nude*, for instance, was auctioned in Paris in 1926, Dr. Claribel paid $6,000 for it—then a substantial sum.

Matisse repaid the Cones' loyalty with the deep but undemonstrative affection that he reserved for people who in his eyes had really proved themselves. This trusted circle was not large, and much of it was English-speaking. It included the English art critics Roger Fry and Clive Bell, the English writer Matthew Stewart Prichard, and the American archeologist Thomas Whittemore, best known for his work in uncovering the splendid mosaics in St. Sophia in Istanbul. Whittemore purchased Matisse's *Terrace, St.-Tropez* in 1909 and presented it to Boston art collector Isabella Stewart Gardner, who turned her home, Fenway Court,

The sporty trio hoisting steins of beer in Munich in 1910 are Matisse, right, the German painter Albert Weisgerber, center, and, at left, Hans Purrmann, whose 1953 self-portrait appears below. One of Matisse's most ardent champions, Purrmann helped organize Matisse's art school in Paris and was its "student manager"; in his native Germany, he arranged Matisse's first one-man show in Berlin, acted as Matisse's agent with German collectors, wrote a series of memoirs about the painter and successfully guided Matisse through three tours of Germany.

into a museum—making *Terrace, St.-Tropez* the first Matisse painting to enter an American museum.

But the patron on whom Matisse leaned most heavily was without a doubt Mrs. Michael Stein. After 1907, when Leo Stein began to weary of Matisse, and Gertrude Stein came more and more to prefer Picasso, Sarah Stein emerged as the member of the family most to be trusted. It was Sarah who took the first Matisse painting across the American continent to San Francisco and started a vogue for Matisse collecting in California. This happened in 1906, after the San Francisco earthquake, when she and her husband went home for a while to attend to their real estate holdings. Among her converts on this trip were Harriet Lane Levy, whose Matisse collection is now in the San Francisco Museum, and Miss Levy's gnomelike little friend Alice B. Toklas, who ultimately followed the Steins to Paris and joined the ménage of Gertrude.

Sarah Stein was also responsible for the short-lived but immensely successful Académie Matisse. She had long been in the habit of showing Matisse her own paintings for correction and, in her typically warm-hearted way, could not resist sharing the privilege. First she invited the German painter Hans Purrmann to join her. Then, when a number of other people expressed a wish to learn from Matisse at first hand, she proposed starting a private art school. Matisse was of two minds about the project. He was touched by his would-be students' enthusiasm, and he remembered what Gustave Moreau's classes had meant to him. But he also feared that it would take time and energy from his own work at a crucial moment in his career. Ever since the close of the fateful Salon d'Automne of 1905, Matisse had been struggling to assimilate a number of unrelated new experiences. Never one to treat such problems lightly, he was finding himself from time to time in serious trouble.

In the winter of 1905-1906, Matisse had gone to Algeria. At Biskra and elsewhere, the light, the color and the relaxed beauty of the local inhabitants had made a deep impression on him. He had noted this briefly in sketches, and then in the following winter at Collioure had worked it into a finished painting, the famous *Blue Nude.* When the *Blue Nude* was shown at the Salon des Indépendants of 1907, it caused another terrible furor. There is certainly something disturbing about the brutish, chunky, naked model, reclining, haunch high in air, in one of Matisse's favorite poses. It is a northern nude in a southern setting: northern for the uncompromising directness of the modeling, the determination to get at the truth no matter how ugly it may seem; southern for the pink shade on the spreading palm leaves and the vibrancy of the color in the shadows.

But *Blue Nude* is also disturbing because in it two different and contradictory sides of Matisse were struggling for mastery. On the one hand there is his desire to model as solidly as possible, to emphasize the three-dimensional character of the subject at hand; on the other hand there is his preoccupation with light, the intense North African light that bleaches color, flattens form and reduces everything to two dimensions. Matisse, who always weighed every move carefully before committing himself, was eddying back and forth between the sculptural and the decorative, the real and the imagined, the direct and the fabricated.

Around this time, too, Matisse was digesting the impressions of his first journey to Italy. In the summer of 1907, he and Madame Matisse visited Venice, Florence, Padua and Siena. Matisse had no particular affection for the High Renaissance; Italian art, as he saw it, was going downhill by the time Leonardo and Michelangelo came to maturity. But he did delight in the earlier Italian painters—Giotto, Duccio, Piero della Francesca. Matisse was far too complex a man to show any immediate influence from this Italian journey, but his reactions were more intense than those of an ordinary visitor. The American artist and art critic Walter Pach, who met Matisse in Italy, wrote that Matisse returned from a day in Arezzo "with enough admiration for the perfect art of Piero della Francesca to last a lifetime."

The third crucial event for Matisse during this period was precipitated by the death of Cézanne, in 1906, and the two memorial shows that followed—an exhibition of 79 watercolors at the Bernheim-Jeune Gallery in June 1907, and a group of 48 paintings in the 1907 Salon d'Automne. Matisse, who had revered Cézanne for more than a decade, must have watched with some irritation as more and more young artists came to share his enthusiasm. Not only did they appear to think that no one had noticed Cézanne before, but they tended to ignore the side of Cézanne that most attracted Matisse. While the younger artists admired those facets of Cézanne's work that foreshadowed Cubism—his injunction, for instance, to "see in nature the cylinder, the sphere, the cone"—Matisse respected Cézanne for the mastery of his "constructions after nature." Every part of a Cézanne painting was as important as every other part; nothing was extraneous. It was this quality that convinced Matisse that Fauvism, with its unpremeditated procedures, was simply not capable of carrying the weight of thought and feeling that he wanted to put into his pictures.

In 1907 Matisse decided to put everything he had into one monumental picture, which he called *Blue Still Life*. The picture was big not so much in size (its dimensions are 35 by 45 inches) as in the fullness and complexity of its intentions. It was in effect an homage to Cézanne on a very grand scale. The subject was one often treated by Cézanne —a table, somewhat aslant the field of vision; a tablecloth, bunched in deep folds and lying half on, half off the table; a still-life arrangement of fruits and bottles and jugs. But where Cézanne usually left much of his canvas open, using a plain wooden tabletop to offset the noble forms of an onion or a peach, Matisse filled up his whole picture with emphatic imagery. He covered his table with a heavily figured cloth and set it against a wallpaper printed with bouquets of flowers; instead of limiting his fruits to a few perfect specimens, he scattered apples, oranges and lemons across the table in rich profusion.

Blue Still Life, while it paid homage to Cézanne, at the same time looked back across Cézanne nearly 300 years, to the Dutch still-life painters of the 17th Century. Jan Davidz. de Heem would have understood Matisse's impulse to heap the plate high, to fill the canvas with succulent objects and rich patterns and textures. De Heem was said to have moved from Utrecht to Antwerp solely because the Antwerp markets contained fruit "in finer condition and state of ripeness to draw from life. . . ."

Matisse never moved from Paris to get better Comice pears—the markets there in any case are as good as any in the world. But he did consistently set a very high value upon the appearance of the things he painted. In the days when he was poor, he often spent more on fruits and flowers than he could really afford. And he always took loving care of his favorite still life objects, even when they were only trumpery tourist souvenirs. His motives could be mistaken for sentiment, except that Matisse himself, as it happens, set the record straight shortly after completing *Blue Still Life*. "To copy the objects in a still life," he said, "is nothing. The painter must strive to render the emotion that the objects awake in him: the emotion of the ensemble, the inter-relation of the objects, the specific character of each object, all interlaced. . . . You must be touched by the tearlike quality of this slender, big-bellied vase and by the generous volume of this copper pot."

He was speaking at the time to the students of his school. The Académie Matisse had finally got going in the early months of 1908. Michael Stein guaranteed it financially, room was found in a former convent on the Rue de Sèvres, the Couvent des Oiseaux, and a large and motley group of students soon formed. Altogether, during the three years the school lasted, it was attended by nearly 120 people, only four of whom were French. The rest were Swedes, Poles, Norwegians, Germans, Hungarians, Americans, Englishmen, an Icelander and a Japanese. Some of them later made names for themselves—Max Weber and Patrick Henry Bruce among the Americans, Béla Czobel among the Hungarians, Matthew Smith among the British. Most of them, however, were people of no particular gifts who would never make a go of it as painters but would be better human beings for having tried.

For something under two dollars a week, the students got the use of the studio and the model, and the certainty of a weekly correction from Matisse. Correction day was Saturday, but Matisse also dropped in during the week when he felt like it or had time. He preferred this informal arrangement—and in fact refused to accept a fee for his corrections—because it would allow him to disengage himself if the school became too great a bother. And a bother in one sense it soon became, for the number of students increased so rapidly that the school had to move almost at once to larger quarters—in another former convent, the Sacré-Coeur, on the Boulevard des Invalides.

Many of the students, knowing Matisse only through his work, expected to find that they could do just what they liked in his classes. On the very first morning, for instance, they welcomed him by festooning the classroom with canvases daubed in the loudest, strongest colors on their palettes. Matisse, walking in, exclaimed, "What's all this rubbish? Take it down at once!" Then he put them through a series of academic exercises that must have made some of them wish they were back in the Beaux-Arts. He insisted on exact measurements, and on the use of the ruler and the plumb line. He forbade them to use color loosely, with-

To the surprise of the students at the Académie Matisse, "the king of the wild beasts" insisted on a serious, academic approach to art, including the discipline of sculpting from a live model *(foreground, above)*. "Note the essential characteristics of the model carefully; they must exist in the complete work, otherwise you have lost your concept on the way," he told them. In this photograph of a sculpture class, Sarah Stein and Hans Purrmann, two co-founders of the school, stand beside Matisse as he criticizes the work of a student.

out regard for other colors. At correction time he could be terrifying: "They got to be as meek as lambs every Saturday," he said later, "and it took all week for me to persuade them to be lions again."

Matisse did not believe that art could be made easy. He had always worked 12 hours a day himself, and he knew of no other way to take art seriously. When he spoke to his students, every word carried the weight of years and years of meditation. Sarah Stein's classroom notes are a uniquely revealing record of how he saw his task. "Lines must never go wild," he would say, "Every line must have its function. . . ." Or again, "Everything must be constructed—built up of parts to make a unit: a tree like a human body, a human body like a cathedral." He advised them to study their subject closely, and then to allow their own feelings to take over: "Close your eyes and hold the vision," he told them, "and then go to work with your own sensibility." Time and again he pointed out to them the kinship between forms, the unexpected parallels: "The pelvis fits into the thighs and suggests an amphora," he said on one occasion. On another, he asked them to notice "the resemblance of this calf to a beautiful vase," or again, to "remark the fullness and olivelike quality of this upper arm."

Matisse learned as much from his teaching experience as any of his pupils. The necessity of putting his thoughts into words, clearly and succinctly, was invaluable to him. In 1908 he carried this process one step further by putting his ideas into writing, in an article for the magazine *La Grande Revue*. From this article, "A Painter's Notes," and from Sarah Stein's classroom notes, it is possible to see into Matisse's mind, to understand the very structure of his thoughts: how he analyzed a figure, broke it down into its parts and then built it up; how he strove to get beyond the initial excitement of painting and enter into the serene state of mind that comes with complete mastery of a subject. To Matisse, the whole point of a work of art was its power to impose itself upon the viewer's imagination: "When I look at the frescoes in Padua," he wrote, "I do not bother to recognize which scene in the life of Christ I have before me. I simply understand, without hesitation, the feeling which comes out of the picture. It's all there, in line, in color, in the composition. The title brings nothing but confirmation."

As for his own art, Matisse hoped it would convey a sense of serenity. "What I dream of is an art of equilibrium," he wrote, "of purity, of tranquility; an art free from disquieting or bothersome subject matter, an art which will calm and soothe the man who works with his head, be he businessman or man of letters." Compared to the evangelical aims of Gauguin or Van Gogh or Munch—painters who were out to change the world—Matisse's aims can be made to seem shallow and frivolous. Some people said that Matisse was simply out to relax the Chairman of the Board at cocktail time. What he had in mind, however, was considerably more profound. When Matisse spoke of an "art of equilibrium," he envisioned an art that evoked an ideal human condition, an image of man at one with himself and at one with his society. In the years immediately before 1914, Matisse achieved this aim—and neither art nor people's concept of art has been quite the same since.

The Brave Collectors

Today all it takes to buy a Matisse is a lot of money. Sixty-odd years ago it was not wealth that was needed so much as courage, faith in the new and a bit of artistic clairvoyance. In the early 1900s, such qualities were almost nonexistent among French collectors and gallery owners, who considered Matisse a misguided radical, hardly a good investment. At his few exhibitions his paintings were jeered at for their implausible colors, two-dimensional quality and primitive design; practically none were bought.

Fortunately for Matisse not everyone shared this disdain. Among the young artists gathered in Paris he was a powerful guiding force, and this enthusiasm communicated itself to a small, and in many ways unlikely, band of collectors—predominantly American and Russian. They bought his art, giving him not only the money he so desperately needed but also the psychological lift of outside encouragement. These brave foreigners were cultured men and women who enjoyed the stimulation of avant-garde Paris. They all had independent means and purchased contemporary art as "amateurs," in the best sense of the word. Though they paid incredibly low prices—$100 or so for a painting that might now bring hundreds of thousands of dollars—they bought from Matisse because they liked and believed in him. They are remembered today as the hardy pioneers who first appreciated the genius of a modern master.

This rugged self-portrait, painted by Matisse when he was 37, was bought by two of his most faithful American collectors, Michael and Sarah Stein. Enchanted with his art, and impressed by his articulateness, Sarah Stein persuaded Matisse to open a school, which she helped to run for about three years.

Self-Portrait, 1906

Henri-Matisse

Michael Stein

Sarah Stein

No American collectors did more to advance the early fortunes of Matisse than a family of eccentric, ruggedly individualistic expatriates, the Steins— elder brother Michael, his wife Sarah, brother Leo and sister Gertrude. At a time when Matisse was being reviled by the French public, the Stein clan bought many paintings, including the ones shown here; and through the Steins, Matisse met other patrons. Leo and Gertrude were flamboyant intellectuals who encouraged writers, poets and painters. But it was with the more retiring, genteel Michael and Sarah that Matisse felt most comfortable.

Joy of Life (study), 1905

Music (sketch), 1907

Three of Matisse's early backers were American spinsters who met him through the Steins. Claribel Cone of Baltimore was strong-willed, one of the first women in America to graduate from medical school. Her sister Etta, and a friend, Harriet Lane Levy of San Francisco, were more moderate. But all three were devoted to Matisse, buying from him confidently and ultimately enriching their hometown museums with their fine collections.

Harriet Levy   *Dr. Claribel Cone*   *Etta Cone*

Girl with Green Eyes, 1909

The Pewter Jug, 1916-1917

Sergei I. Shchukin

ARussian textile importer with a passionate craving for modern art provided Matisse with some of his largest early sales and several important commissions. Sergei Shchukin was born to a very wealthy, art-buying family—his four brothers had built a fine collection of old masters. But Sergei had an eye for the new and different. The walls of his 18th Century rococo palace in Moscow were covered with daring modern art, and he was not afraid to buy the abjured work of Matisse. Indeed, so eager was he for Matisse's pictures that he sometimes claimed them even before the paint was dry. But the prescience that led Shchukin to collect Matisses won him little respect in the art world: in Paris he was snidely branded "the mad Russian."

Harmony in Red, 1908-1909

Madame Matisse, 1913

The Painter's Family, 1911

Conversation, 1909

Shchukin fell so in love with Matisse's art that in 1909 he commissioned two giant canvases, *Music* and *Dance* (*below*). Each was about 12 feet long and was intended to decorate a landing along the stairway in the importer's Moscow home. As the theme for *Dance*, Matisse returned to his monumental *Joy of Life*, extracting a circle of gay dancers from the background. For that scene and for this new work the artist drew on his memories of the Catalan dance-in-the-round called the *sardana*, which he had seen in southern France. But while the *sardana* is intricate and mathematical in its precision, Matisse invested it with joyful exuberance. *Dance* is so vital that it repeatedly

startled the artist—as it hung in his studio the rays of the setting sun made it seem to quiver. He had gone all out to intensify his color, saying later that he had aimed at "the bluest of blues for the sky, the greenest of greens for the earth, and a vibrant vermilion for the bodies."

For *Music*, Matisse also went back to an earlier work (*page 83*). There, two of the listeners are so stirred by the music that they have begun dancing. Here, however, he emphasized their rapt concentration, their absorption in private thoughts. Stillness has replaced action, creating a sharp counterpoint to the frenzy of *Dance*.

In these works, Matisse's drawing is deliberately simple,

unencumbered by traditional modeling and tricks of
perspective. He said of these paintings, "We are moving
toward serenity by simplifying ideas and figures. The
whole is to be our only ideal."

Matisse eventually traveled to Moscow to hang these
pictures in Shchukin's palace, where they remained until
the Soviet revolution engulfed Russia in 1917. Shchukin
escaped to France, but all his art was confiscated. And
ironically, Soviet Russia, which officially frowns on
abstract art, became heir to some of the best Matisses.
Today, in the Hermitage Museum, *Dance* and *Music* are
displayed in the perspective duplicated below.

Dance and *Music*, 1910

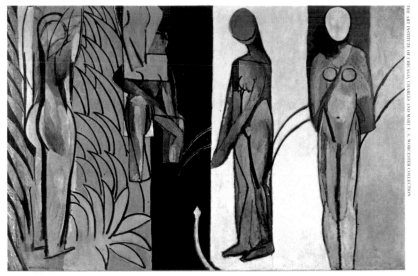

Bathers by a River, 1916-1917

During the time that Matisse was being discovered by foreign collectors, he painted some pictures that he did not sell. He did not even exhibit the two paintings shown here until many years after he had completed them. Although he never explained why he held them back, it may have been that Matisse wanted, or needed, to keep them because each represented a significant experience in his life.

Both pictures were finished while Europe was deeply embroiled in World War I, and art life as it had been known ceased to exist. Exhibitions were few, French collectors fewer still, and Matisse's contacts with his foreign patrons were more and more difficult to maintain. Under these circumstances, he was able to work for several years on paintings that were both too large and too difficult for any existing market. *Bathers by a River (above)* is just under 13 feet long. It may have been partly inspired by a Cézanne painting of a similar subject that Matisse had owned for many years, but just as likely it relates to the landscape of North Africa, a pleasant reminiscence of the visits the artist had made earlier. The sword-edged foliage, the intense contrasts of light and shade and the cryptic and potentially dangerous snake recall the African environment in subtle ways. *The Moroccans (right)* is a more direct and beguiling evocation of the colorful land that he had come to love during his visits in 1912 and 1913. The painting, the most abstract work he had yet done, is composed in three sections: at the upper left, beneath a typically North African skyline, is a terrace with potted flowers; below, fat melons droop on leafy vines; at the right, a few robed Moroccans, as solid as architecture, are crouching. The painting requires study to appreciate everything Matisse has put into it—and left out. When asked to explain, however, he said only: "I find it difficult to describe this painting of mine with words. It is the beginning of my expression with color, with blacks and their contrasts."

The Moroccans, 1916

V

The Light of Nice

By 1909 Matisse had an assured market for his pictures and a reputation that was growing steadily—at least outside his native France. (French enthusiasm for his work, when expressed at all, stopped well short of signing a check.) He had the lively support of a group of open-minded Americans; Scandinavians by the score attended his school; and through his friendship with the German painter Hans Purrmann a number of his paintings had found their way into German collections and into Berlin's Cassirer Gallery where, in the winter of 1908-1909, he had a one-man show. Among those who knew his work, Matisse, just then pushing 40, was regarded as the major painter of the day. Gertrude Stein wrote that his German pupils sent him cases of Rhine wine and "a very fine black police dog, the first of the breed that any of us had seen." Thomas Whittemore, the American archeologist, marked the opening of the Cassirer show in Berlin by sending him a gigantic laurel wreath—a gesture to which Matisse responded characteristically. "But I'm not dead yet," he said. Meanwhile, Madame Matisse appropriated the red ribbon from the wreath for her daughter's hair and used some of the laurel leaves to flavor the soup.

With this increasing notice Matisse was finding it more and more irksome to live, as it were, over the shop. Although his home and studio were now in one of the grandest houses in Paris, the former convent of the Sacré Coeur, the fact of having his school so near at hand meant that his teaching obligations, real or imagined, were continually preying on his mind. He began to look around for another place to live and work, and in the summer of 1909 he found it. The new home was a villa at Issy-les-Moulineaux, now only 15 minutes by taxi from the center of Paris, but then completely countrified. The house was a square, two-storied affair that sat in a large garden with a pond, a hothouse and some serpentine paths between neatly trimmed patches of lawn. It had a view over woodlands and orchards of apple and pear—and it had a bathroom, a touch of modernity that Gertrude Stein claimed the Matisses learned to appreciate only "from long contact with Americans," although she hastened to add that the Matisses had

Of the many interior scenes with a view through an open window that Matisse painted, this is one of the finest. Painted from his room in the Hôtel Beau-Rivage in Nice, the picture documents Matisse's fascination with the brilliant Mediterranean light and the sharp contrasts it produces. Against the dazzling sea, the shuttered window and interior walls are black, while the painter's beloved violin glows like a jewel in its blue-lined case.

Interior with a Violin, 1917-1918

always been "scrupulously neat and clean." In any case, the house was, and still is today, a genuine little country house almost within walking distance of the amenities of Paris. Matisse, who only five years before had been desperately poor, referred to this miniature estate as "our little Luxembourg."

One of the first things Matisse ordered for Issy-les-Moulineaux was a large prefabricated shed to serve as a garden studio. He bought it at the suggestion of a new American friend, the photographer Edward Steichen, but the need for it was created by a commission from another international acquaintance, the Russian collector Sergei Shchukin. Within a short time Shchukin was to become the most important of all Matisse's patrons. He was not much to look at, a small, rather timorous man with a disproportionately large head and an expression that an unkind friend called piglike. Neither was he much to talk to, at least at first meeting, for he was afflicted with a bad stammer that distressed other people as much as it hindered Shchukin. But he did have three assets as a collector, two of them personal and the third an accident of environment. He had an infallible eye, and he was unboundedly rich. Perhaps more important, he belonged to a society that had no history in matters of art. Russia in a sense had leaped directly from medieval religious art to 18th Century realism—mostly on the orders of Peter the Great. Consequently when Shchukin began

In the Moscow mansion of Sergei Shchukin, one salon alone contained some 20 of the 37 major Matisse paintings that the rich merchant owned. The section of this "Matisse" room that appears below shows a part of the great 20th Century art collection as it was hung in the sumptuous 18th Century rococo interior of Shchukin's home in prerevolutionary Russia.

to collect art, he did so without inbred prejudices or preconceptions.

For more than a decade before his meeting with Matisse, Shchukin had been demonstrating the excellence of his eye. At a time when most Frenchmen would not have modern paintings as gifts, he was buying Gauguin, Cézanne and Renoir, and was even collecting such little-known artists as Édouard Vuillard, Odilon Redon and Henri Rousseau. No one could say where the money for these purchases came from, still less how much of it there was. But it was known that Shchukin was in the business of buying and selling things that were much in demand, from the best tea to the most sumptuous textiles. And presumably he bought them cheap and sold them dear, for his fortune appeared to have no visible limit.

The thing Shchukin most enjoyed was to board the express train that steamed majestically southwest from Moscow to Paris, and upon its arrival several days later to head straight for the galleries. He had a genuine and private passion for pictures. For Leo Stein, a painting was an excuse for an impromptu talk that would last as long as he had an audience; for Shchukin, it was an inspiration to silence and concentration. Sir Kenneth Clark once observed that few people could look at a painting for longer than it took to peel an orange and eat it; Shchukin was one of the few exceptions. He could look at a picture for hours on end and go on getting more out of it.

To this natural love for painting, Shchukin added enthusiasm and purpose derived from civic pride. He was one of the leaders in a small group of wealthy Muscovites who wanted to see Moscow replace St. Petersburg as the cultural capital of Russia. Compared to genteel St. Petersburg, Moscow was a rough, dirty, competitive city, a place for doing business and making money. It was defiantly hostile to the imitation-European style of life that flourished in St. Petersburg—to the English gardens and governesses, the French food, the Germanic earnestness in matters of education and art. While St. Petersburg looked outward to Western Europe for its inspiration, Moscow looked inward to its own Eastern tradition, to the folk art, the icons, the legends and lore of Russia itself.

Shchukin and the other members of what could be called the Muscovite Enlightenment set out to tap this tradition and produce an all-Russian approach to the arts. Without them, there would have been no Russian opera, no naturalistic Russian theater, no revolution in Russian stage design. One of their number, the railroad millionaire Savva Mamontov, singlehandedly affected the future of music, architecture, the theater and painting. Mamontov turned his country estate into a workshop for Russian arts and crafts, financed a theater and commissioned Russian artists to redesign the costumes and settings for its productions, underwrote the modernization of the Moscow opera and added to its roster such great artists as Feodor Chaliapin. When the Czar's art commissioners refused to show the work of a young Russian painter, Mikail Vrubel, because he was "too modern" Mamontov built a special pavilion just to house a Vrubel exhibition.

Mamontov's motives were largely altruistic. He wanted to raise professional standards, heighten the general awareness of Russia's ancestral energies and make life richer and more invigorating for everyone. In a less comprehensive way, this was Shchukin's ambition too. His house in central Moscow—a brilliantly ornamented, quasi-Oriental mansion—was thrown open to the public for chamber music concerts, and anyone who wanted to see his collection of paintings was welcome. Those who came got a better idea of contemporary French art than any museum could have given them. The 14 Gauguin paintings that hung in Shchukin's dining room are still the finest group of Gauguins, public or private, anywhere in the world.

Shchukin bought his first Matisse painting around 1904, and several years later met the artist at Leo and Gertrude Stein's. He was slower than the Steins to appreciate the first Fauve paintings, but he very soon overtook the Steins—and indeed everyone else—in his enthusiasm for Matisse at his most radical. In this, he had one advantage. Unlike Matisse's Western patrons, he did not relate Matisse's work to the traditions of Western European art. In Russia those traditions did not apply. When Matisse dropped modeling and perspective, Shchukin was not affronted: the great Russian icon painters of the 14th and 15th Centuries had not bothered with them either. When Matisse built up his paintings from flat areas of strong color, Shchukin rejoiced; the icon painters had worked that way too. He rejoiced again, and for the same reason, when Matisse embedded his human figures, mosaiclike, into their background. And when Matisse introduced elements of Islamic design into his work, Shchukin got the point at once, for Russian and Islamic art have a natural affinity.

Shchukin was the ideal patron for Matisse and he appeared at exactly the right time. Matisse was just embarking on what he later called "the period of new acquisitions." It was his private phrase for the new experiences that were coming to him through travel and for the new ways of expressing himself that were coming to him through years of meditation. But the phrase could have applied equally well to acquisitions of quite another sort. From being known to the general public primarily through abusive messages scrawled on Montmartre walls ("Matisse will drive you crazy! Matisse is worse than absinthe!"), he was suddenly being recognized as a much-debated but indispensable figure in the international art world. He was given a small show at the Alfred Stieglitz Gallery in New York early in 1908, and around the same time took part in a group show in London. In the spring of 1908 he contributed to an exhibition of recent French painting in Moscow, and in the winter of 1908-1909 came his large one-man show at the Cassirer Gallery in Berlin. His Scandinavian students mounted a show of his work in Stockholm in 1909 that reverberated through Scandinavia for more than a decade.

All this sounds splendid, but in fact it was offset in almost every case by the hatred, envy and brutish indifference of officialdom, of the press and even of fellow artists. When Matisse went to Berlin for the opening of his show in the Cassirer Gallery, the experience was uncompromisingly hideous. The show itself was something of a fiasco; hostility

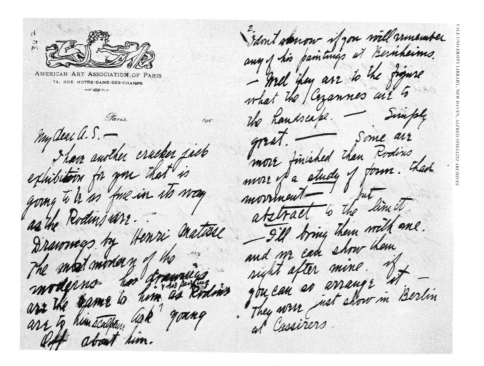

"I have another cracker-jack exhibition for you . . . Drawings by Henri Matisse, the most modern of the moderns . . . Simply great"; thus wrote the American photographer and aspiring painter Edward Steichen to his friend and mentor Alfred Stieglitz in New York. A pioneer of artistic photography, Stieglitz was also a champion of avant-garde art of all kinds, and his gallery on New York's Fifth Avenue was to introduce the American public to most of the great modern painters and sculptors. On April 6, 1908, Stieglitz opened a show of "Drawings, Lithographs, Watercolors and Etchings by M. Henri Matisse of Paris," the first public exhibition of the painter in the United States.

to it was so widespread that the paintings were taken down as soon as Matisse was safely on his way home. Not one of the artists or critics associated with the modern movement—and Berlin had its fair share of such men—would come out for Matisse. Even the most favorable review ended with the comment that the one response to all the pictures was "a huge, irrepressible impulse to laugh!" Small wonder that Matisse, walking the streets of Berlin, felt as if the glowering façades might reach down and gobble him up.

In London and New York the reviews of his work were equally discouraging, although he was spared the anguish of being there in person. In London, the critic for *The Burlington Magazine* observed that "with M. Matisse, motive and treatment alike are infantile," and the critic for the New York *Evening Mail* wrote that Matisse's female figures were "of an ugliness that seems to condemn this man's brain to the limbo of artistic degeneration." Even the most sophisticated American critic of the day, James Gibbons Huneker, took issue with Matisse, describing his studies from the naked model as "memoranda of the gutter and the brothel." And *The Nation*'s anonymous report from Paris on the 1908 Salon d'Automne called Matisse's paintings "direct insults to the eye and understanding."

At this point, Matisse unexpectedly got support from the great panjandrum of the Old Masters, the art critic and historian Bernard Berenson. Writing to *The Nation* in response to its article, Berenson observed that Matisse, far from being a common fraud, had "after 20 years of very earnest searching at last found the great highroad traveled by all the best masters of the visual arts for the last 60 centuries at least. Indeed he is singularly like them in every essential respect. He is a magnificent draftsman and a great designer. Of his color I do not venture to speak. Not that it displeases me—far from it. But I can better understand its failing to charm at first; for color is something we . . . are still singularly uncertain of—we are easily frightened by the slightest divergence from the habitual."

Berenson was right about Matisse's use of color. It did indeed diverge from the habitual, and it did so more and more as Matisse learned to exploit his "new acquisitions." From his travels in North Africa, for instance, he had carried away a memory of the effect of intense light on color and volume. In Europe, where the light is grudging and inconstant, painters for centuries had worked in terms of volumes charted in minute detail by modeling and deep shadow. But in Africa the strong light flattened volume and wiped out the subtle indentations of a brick wall or the folds of a garment. When one walks down the street of a North African city, the prospect composes itself into a series of brightly colored areas, some of them patterned, some of them plain, but all of them resolutely flat.

Matisse was not the first painter to notice this, but he was the first to adapt it completely to his own purposes. He had tried long and loyally to reproduce the color effects of the Old Masters—tried, that is, to use color in ways that related to universal experience. But now he was 40, old enough to risk taking painting into a new phase. What he wanted to do was set color free, release it from its role as assistant and enlist it as an equal partner. "Color was not given to us in order that we should imitate Nature," he told a friend. "It was given to us so that we can express our own emotions."

He also wanted to free art from the subterfuge of perspective. For centuries European painters had gone to infinite trouble to convince the public that a painting was a thing to look into, a window on a world that existed in depth, just like the view outside a real window. But painters had not always worked in this way. In Islamic art, in prehistoric cave painting, in the panel paintings and frescoes of 12th and 13th Century Europe, this preoccupation with perspective did not exist. No one had tried to impose the order of everyday experience upon the facts set down in the picture—and the curious thing is that while classical perspective now looks dated and contrived, the earlier works do not. There is something fresh, spontaneous and timeless about a Persian miniature or a Dordogne cave painting, or the altarpiece in a medieval cathedral. A painting, when all is said and done, is simply a flat surface. "All right, so it's flat," Matisse's new paintings were to say. "It's flat, why don't we admit it?"

One of the first paintings in which he tried this new approach was *Harmony in Red*, a picture whose musical title cannot have been wholly accidental. "I wanted," Matisse said later, "to work with areas of flat color, and I wanted to place those areas of flat color as a composer places his chords." Matisse, who played the violin, was enough of a musician to know what he was talking about. Doubtless he had in mind the ease and assurance with which a great composer signals the change of mood in a musical passage with just two or three chords. Music, in this respect, moves more swiftly and strikes deeper than any of the other arts. It also happens to be especially effective at conjuring up the idea of earthly paradise—an idea that also underlay many of Matisse's finest paintings.

Shchukin bought *Harmony in Red* straight from the studio, even before it was exhibited. At the time he bought it, its dominant color was not red at all, but blue, and at an earlier stage it had been green. Matisse probably settled on the final color, a particularly vibrant cherry red, because it heightened the sense of vitality and well-being that he meant the picture to convey. Fundamentally *Harmony in Red (page 86)* is a reworking of a classic French theme—the table containing the last vestiges of a good meal. Matisse himself had used this theme at least twice before, in *Breton Serving Girl (page 24)* in 1896 and in *The Dinner Table (pages 24-25)* in 1897. Once again there are some half-emptied carafes of wine, a chair or two, a servant bending over the table and a suggestion of a landscape through an open window. Once again the scene is pervaded by a sense of bourgeois comfort. People have sat at this table and have had a thundering good time, and now the servant—quick-tongued and competent in the great tradition of French servants—will do the dishes. Everything is just as it should be.

But in *Harmony in Red*, the good life is suggested not so much by things as by color. Where *The Dinner Table* used fine china and glass and "period" chairs to convey a sense of richness and earthly fulfillment, *Harmony in Red* makes the point with an imperious, all-enveloping red. Indeed the painting seems at first a great flat sheet of this color. On closer examination the sheet is seen to fold where the tabletop meets the wall, and to fold a second time where the tablecloth falls over the edge of the table. But Matisse has minimized these changes in plane by covering both the wall and the table with the same decorative pattern. It is a traditional French pattern called a *toile de jouy*, and its basic motif is a basket of flowers framed in a serpentine line that is meant to represent garlands of foliage—but could just as well be taken for a particularly luxuriant pair of antlers.

The view through the window is equally flat. It is a spring landscape, with new green leaves on the bushes, flowers in the grass and a thin powdering of late snow over the blossoming fruit trees. But no modeling of form, no modulation of light, defines the lay of the land. Instead of using perspective to build his composition, Matisse used a series of pictorial analogies. The roof of a house seen beyond the window is identical to the shape of a chair seat in the foreground. The sinuous branching of the trees in the garden is echoed in the antler forms of the fabric on the table and wall. The flower stems in the fabric are sketched in with the same economical, abbreviated line as the servant's hair. Most of all, however, *Harmony in Red* is held together by its chords of pure color —full, sonorous, perfectly even, conveying just the effect Matisse intended.

Shchukin put *Harmony in Red* on his dining-room wall, at right angles to a long line of Gauguins. He went on buying Matisse's work throughout 1908, but at the same time he began to talk to him about a special commission. During his visits to the Steins', Shchukin had noticed a little picture by Matisse called *Music*, dated 1907. Its subject was similar to that of *Joy of Life*, but it had none of the larger picture's elaborate plotting and planning. At the left stood a naked man, playing a violin; in the lower right sat a figure listening to the music; behind them in the middle ground, two female figures were locked in a Thurber-esque dance routine. It was an oddly incomplete painting—Matisse expressly called it a sketch—but something about its forthright sculptural style suggested to Shchukin that Matisse might be the very man to do a wall decoration he contemplated for the stairwell of his home. He mentioned the project to Matisse, and Matisse was interested: during the winter of 1908 he produced an almost full-size sketch for a mural that he called *Dance (page 88)*.

Matisse's sculpture *La Serpentine*, which appears in Edward Steichen's romantic photograph of the artist below, is a perfect example of the simplification of form that he strove for. He was obviously uninterested in a conventionally beautiful human figure, and he wrote that he had "thinned and composed the forms so that the movement would be comprehensible from all points of view." Vilified even by the model who posed for it—"How awfully ugly!" she said—the work superbly accomplishes Matisse's purpose.

The subject of his sketch was five people engaged in a round dance. Their bodies were a pleasant sandy color, faintly tinged with pink from the physical exertion, but they were not too immersed in their activity to look around and judge the effect they were making. Dance was very much in the air in Paris at the time—Sergei Diaghilev's Russian Ballet was about to give its first Western European season, and Isadora Duncan was at the height of her fame. Matisse apparently took note of all this, but his own composition stays faithful to his memory of an unspoiled peasant dance. *Dance* is based on a group of figures in the background of *Joy of Life*, and they in turn were based on a Catalan round dance which Matisse had seen fishermen perform in the evening on the beach at Collioure.

Shchukin was so pleased with the sketch that he whisked Matisse off to the Restaurant Larue—then, as now, one of the best restaurants in Paris—to talk to him about an even more ambitious project. Instead of one wall decoration for his stairwell, he proposed that Matisse do three, one for each landing. Each, as Matisse explained later to a friend, was to be different in feeling. "On the first, I want the visitor to be stimulated and have a feeling of lightness. My first panel represents, therefore, the dance: a round dance whirling above the hills. On the next floor, the silent heart of the house, I see a musical scene, with a group of attentive listeners. On the third floor all is peace, and I shall paint a scene of repose, with people lying on the grass, talking or dreaming." All three were to convey emotion directly, by the simplest possible means: *Dance* was to have only three colors, "blue for the sky, pink for the bodies, green for the hill. . . ."

Shchukin sent Matisse a firm order from Moscow for *Dance* and also placed an order for the second panel, *Music*. The price set for *Dance* was 15,000 francs (then worth about $3,000), and for *Music*, 12,000 francs. The double commission was by far Matisse's largest single transaction to date. It was, in fact, a turning point in his career. But all did not go smoothly. Matisse might have foreseen trouble when Shchukin wrote him from Moscow of his resolve "to brave the opinion of our local bourgeoisie by hanging on my staircase a picture with NUDES in it." But Matisse failed to sense the warning. In the final version of *Dance* the nakedness of the dancers is in fact accentuated: Matisse stressed the dance's innate ferocity, made the bodies brick red and added a note almost of desperation to the scene. For instance, in the sketch the second dancer on the left was a pleasantly plump girl who looked as if she was rather enjoying the workout, but in the final version the exertion looks as if it might kill her off. Altogether *Dance* is closer in spirit to Stravinsky's *Rite of Spring*, in which death ends the dance, than to wholesome recreation.

In *Dance* Matisse drew upon his memory of the dancing of Collioure fishermen, but in *Music (page 89)*, he invented everything from scratch except the figure of the standing fiddler (which he lifted from the little sketch, *Music*, owned by the Steins). He wanted to suggest a music of stillness and trance, quite the opposite of the thumping and pounding of the music suggested by *Dance*. To achieve this, he placed the fiddler off to one edge of the canvas and gave him a withdrawn, inward-looking pose. Next to him he placed a seated flute player, with one leg folded so that it lay at right angles to the fiddler. From a distance the two figures seem to interlock, creating a single, abstract unit. The nature of the music is implicit in their pose, but as music also needs to be heard, Matisse added three listeners. At first they were conventional music lovers, lounging on the hillside in attitudes of conventional rapture, and there were flowers and an enraptured dog. But as the work progressed, Matisse eliminated the flowers and dog and dispensed with the listeners' esthetic, skyward-looking poses. Instead he sat them bolt upright, knees drawn up against their bodies, in attitudes of intense concentration; each ignores the others, absorbed in his own private happiness.

Shchukin was delighted with both pictures, but his enthusiasm for them conflicted with what he regarded as his obligations to society. He had two adopted teen-age daughters, and his chamber music concerts drew large numbers of women as well as men—how could he possibly have pictures of naked men and women all over the stairs? Especially when, as in *Music*, the facts of manhood were so explicitly spelled out? Shchukin foresaw himself ostracized and his daughters barred from society. A contract was a contract, but Shchukin had to live in Moscow and Matisse did not. Would Matisse take back the paintings and redo them, one-third size, so that Shchukin could hang them in his own private apartments, where no one would be the wiser? Matisse was appalled: so much so, in fact, that he dropped everything and went off to Spain for three months, determined to forget the whole thing.

When he returned to Issy-les-Moulineaux, in January 1911, he began work at once on a group of paintings completely different in character from the wall decorations he had been doing for Shchukin. They were crammed with incident, astir with brilliant mosaics of color, diversified almost to the point of incoherence. The inspiration for them had come from another of Matisse's "new acquisitions." In the previous summer he had gone to Munich to see a large exhibition of Islamic art. It was one of the great events of his life. He had come away confirmed in his belief that one did not have to be trapped in the squirrel cage of conventional Western perspective: the world could be flattened out, tilted upward, set free from the limitations of normal vision. Narrative, ornament and significant detail could be combined into complex pictures that made sense on every level—as records of events, as studies of character, as beautiful objects. It had been done before; it could be done again.

The first of the pictures to use this "new acquisition" was *The Paint-*

er's *Family (page 87)*, in which Madame Matisse and the three children are placed like paper cutouts against a background coruscated with densely patterned color. Carpets, wallpaper, upholstery fabric, even the tiles that frame the fireplace—everything is on the move. This was followed by *Interior with Eggplants*, a picture so full of pattern that it seems at first to be one huge, flower-spattered carpet. The walls, the floor and the painted frame within the real frame are all covered with the same insistent pattern of polka dots arranged in circles. To compound the problem, Matisse added a scroll-patterned folding screen, more scrolls on a tablecloth and several mirrors to reflect all these patterns back and forth.

In another revolutionary painting, *The Red Studio*, he took the opposite tack. Instead of heaping pattern upon pattern, he reduced the walls and floor of his workroom to one continuous sheet of uniform red. Yet the room reads as a room because of the subtle way Matisse has laid in its furnishings. Some of them are obviously against a back wall, others are just as obviously against a side wall, aslant the field of vision. And though none of them is painted in three dimensions, all of them appear to have bulk because of the relationship in which they stand to one another.

Meanwhile, as Matisse investigated these "new acquisitions" from Islamic art, Shchukin was having second thoughts about *Music* and *Dance*. Deciding that it was absurd to forgo two such beautiful paintings, he had them packed up and shipped to Moscow in January 1911. At the same time he invited Matisse to come to Moscow to supervise their hanging, and Matisse accepted. Ostensibly it was to be a private visit, but from the moment Matisse stepped off the train in the fall of 1911, he was surrounded by admirers. Reporters interviewed him on the station platform and followed him everywhere, and an eager public hung on his every word. Moscow knew of him not only through his pictures at Shchukin's and an exhibition, several years before, of modern French painting, but through his own article, "A Painter's Notes," which had been translated and published in a Moscow literary magazine, *The Golden Fleece*.

When Matisse got to Shchukin's house, he found that his pictures were hanging in tiers against damasked walls, in competition with an oppressive amount of ornament—coved and decorated ceilings, imitation Baroque doorways, sumptuous and heavily swagged valances that reached halfway to the floor, candelabra heavy enough to stun an elephant. It was a setting that would have overwhelmed less powerful paintings. Nevertheless, after Matisse persuaded Shchukin to remove the paintings' glass coverings and to hang them flush with the wall instead of tilted downward, they held their own quite easily.

Shchukin was a sensitive and considerate host, and he saw to it that Matisse got the most out of Moscow. He had been quick to recognize Matisse's interest in non-European art, and he must have foreseen with what excitement Matisse would respond to Moscow's 15th Century icons. A collection of these icons had recently been cleaned and restored, and they stood revealed for the first time in centuries in their full glory. Even allowing for the politeness of a much-feted visitor, Matisse was clearly astonished by them. "You Russians," he said, "don't realize what treasures you possess. . . . Young people here have at their disposal examples of art which are far finer than those available to young people in Europe. It is here in Moscow that new discoveries are to be made. Modern artists should draw inspiration from these early Russians. . . ."

Some Russian scholars have suggested that Matisse himself drew inspiration from the icons and that *The Painter's Family* was directly influenced by them. The truth is that *The Painter's Family* was almost complete months before Matisse left for Moscow. But Matisse and the icon painters undeniably had certain things in common: an interest in the expressive power of the arabesque line, a love of pure, singing color, a fastidious regard for outline drawing, and the knowledge that, as Matisse put it, "exactitude is not truth." Like Matisse, the icon painters habitually tilted space upward toward the observer; like him, they reveled in the beauty and solemnity of the paint surface. And that surface in 1911 must have been enough to make Matisse fall in love with painting all over again, for the icons had just been cleaned of more than four centuries of candle soot, over-painting and ill-judged varnishing.

Like all visitors to Moscow, Matisse was impressed by the ancient buildings in the Kremlin, and he longed to paint them in the snow. But the snow came late in the winter of 1911, and he was anxious to get back to his studio. In November he left Moscow, never to return. His influence, however, remained strong for more than a decade. Russia's artists and intellectuals remembered him as a man who would risk anything to remain true to his own private vision; whenever free spirits met together, Matisse's name entered the conversation more often than that of any other European artist.

For Matisse, the influence of Russia was equally strong, although its effects were not immediately apparent. The icon painters had confirmed many of his own ideas, not least of them, his ideas about space. When Matisse painted the legs of a dancer, for instance, he was as concerned about the shape of the space between the legs as he was about the legs themselves. Looking at the work of the icon painters, he saw that they too were aware of this: that the space between the upraised arms of a Virgin, or between the figures of the Trinity, was an important element in the painting.

Matisse's trip to Russia was the last of the great journeys during the period of "new acquisitions." Thereafter, except for two journeys to Morocco in the winters of 1911 and 1912, he did not leave France again until 1930, when he went to Tahiti. The Moroccan visits were purely for pleasure. Matisse loved North Africa for itself—the unending sunshine, the riot of flowers, the unhurried magnificence of the Berber tribesmen. He also loved it because it made palpable a way of life he delighted to paint. It was a way of life in which flowers did not have to be bought, but were there for the picking; in which people did not dress up, but dressed gorgeously as a matter of course; in which the intensity of the light was a fact, not a thing that had to be imagined. Altogether, he felt enormously well in North Africa, and at home, too, he had reasons for being pleased with life.

There were signs that the message of his paintings was at last getting through to the public. Although French officialdom still failed to understand him (Apollinaire, describing the opening of the 1913 Salon d'Automne, wrote that the attending Minister listened with obvious boredom to a eulogy of Matisse), Matisse already had the next best thing to official recognition. Four years before, in September 1909, Bernheim-Jeune, one of the great galleries of Paris, had signed a contract with him. Under it, Bernheim-Jeune agreed to buy Matisse's entire output at prices ranging from $100 to $400 a painting—basing the amount, as was usual, upon the picture's dimensions rather than on its quality. This contract had been negotiated by Félix Fénéon, the friend and champion of Seurat, and it was the first of a series that was to cover every year between 1909 and 1926, except for a two-year interruption during World War I. Bernheim-Jeune's support meant security of a more or less impregnable sort and access to a large, international art-buying public.

Matisse's best customer, however, continued to be his Russian patron, Shchukin, who went on buying most of Matisse's major paintings until the outbreak of World War I. Toward the end Shchukin was seconded by his friend and fellow-collector, Ivan Morosov. In April 1913, for instance, when Bernheim-Jeune put on a show of Matisse's Moroccan paintings, Shchukin and Morosov between them bought eight of the 12 pictures. One result of this Russian enthusiasm was that for 40 years or more, some of Matisse's best work was unknown in the West, or was known only by hearsay. Not until the 1950s did the Russian government finally put its Matisse paintings on public display. Even now, access to them is something of an adventure: they are on the top floor of the Hermitage Museum in Leningrad, in what used to be the preserve of the Czarina's ladies-in-waiting.

For that matter it was an adventure to see Matisse's paintings even when they were still in Shchukin's house. In October 1913, Shchukin wrote Matisse that 10 museum directors had come to Moscow in the preceding two weeks expressly to see his pictures. They had come from Berlin, Frankfurt, Nuremberg, Hagen, Strasbourg, Flensburg, Hamburg, Darmstadt, Halle and Oslo—and every one of them had spoken of Matisse as "a great master." Earlier, in February 1913, 250,000 Americans had poured into the 69th Regiment Armory in New York to look at a special exhibition of modern art, the largest such collection yet assembled in the United States. It included 13 Matisse paintings, three of his drawings and a large sculpture. But there the response had been different. Although the Armory Show's most discussed painting was Marcel Duchamp's *Nude Descending a Staircase*, it was Matisse's work that most consistently attracted violent comments from the press. "An art essentially epileptic"... "Ugly, coarse, narrow, revolting"... "Making insanity pay"... "The drawings of a nasty boy," were some of the typical comments.

The New York Times, which had been one of Matisse's harshest critics, was nevertheless sufficiently impressed by the uproar to send a lady reporter to Issy-les-Moulineaux to interview him. To her great surprise, she found "not a long-haired, slovenly dressed, eccentric man, as I had imagined, but a fresh, healthy, robust blonde gentleman. . . whose simple and unaffected cordiality put me directly at my ease. . . . One's ideas of the man and of his work are entirely opposed to one another: the latter abnormal to the last degree, and the man an ordinary, healthy individual such as one meets by the dozen every day. . . ." Matisse, anxious to reinforce her impression, asked her to "tell the American people that I am a normal man; that I am a devoted husband and father, that I have three fine children, that I go to the theater, ride horseback, have a comfortable home, a fine garden that I love, flowers, etc., just like any man."

He need not have worried. Before the year was out Matisse had acquired two new and important American patrons, the New York lawyer John Quinn and the Philadelphia patent-medicine (Argyrol) millionaire Albert Barnes. Quinn, who had been one of the sponsors of the Armory Show, soon afterward bought *The Blue Nude* and the small sketch, *Music*, from Leo and Gertrude Stein. Barnes was already a collector of Impressionists and post-Impressionists, and eventually assembled the greatest Matisse collection in America. They were to be followed, at a respectful distance, by scores of other American enthusiasts. At long last everything was going Matisse's way, and the signs were there for anyone to see. The house and the garden at Issy-les-Moulineaux began to look like one of his own fastidious, well-appointed pictures: trim and gleaming and well ordered. There were Cézannes on the dining-room wall, and the garden, tended by a gardener, overflowed with a superabundance of fine flowers. Matisse had it made.

Riding with his children—Jean is at the right, Pierre and Marguerite at the left—in the fields of Clamart, near Paris, Matisse seems like any average father. An enthusiastic rider, Matisse often went out alone, with the children, or with his friend Picasso who sometimes joined him during the time he lived in the suburbs. But, as always, diversions from his work were rare: it was at about this time that Matisse was painting the large-scale compositions *Dance* and *Music* for his Russian patron Shchukin, finishing his sculpture *La Serpentine* and beginning dozens of other pictures.

By the end of World War I, Matisse had gained prominence as an artist, his children had grown up and, in his late forties, he had every reason to regard his life with quiet satisfaction. During the easy and prosperous decade that followed, he turned to a subject that was a symbol of rich pleasure, the languorous, sensual women of the harem, the odalisques. Matisse had seen many North African women during his earlier travels. Now he recaptured their sumptuous beauty with the help of pretty models, whom he posed naked or partly dressed in filmy, brightly colored costumes.

The tradition of painting odalisques was a long and respected one in French art; Ingres, Delacroix and Renoir had established it. But Matisse's infatuation with these indolent playthings is unexpected—he was, after all, a precise painter concerned with exact color harmonies and meticulous composition. This intellectual bent was only one side of his nature, however, and in his odalisque paintings he revealed himself as a man who loved the idea of pleasure and delighted in the exotic. While indulging his enchantment with the odalisques, he nevertheless continued to press forward. He experimented again with sculpture and lithography in portraying these lovely women, and in his paintings of them he aimed to compress space into flatter planes, to fill the entire surface of the canvas with a unified decorative pattern and to achieve ever more exciting interactions of color.

The Languid Odalisques

This lithograph of an odalisque, made by Matisse in 1925, repeats a pose that the artist interpreted in a variety of prints, drawings and sculpture as well as painting. In all media, Matisse followed his rule that "the simplest methods are those which best allow the painter to express himself."

Odalisque in Striped Pantaloons, 1925

8/10 epr d'artiste   Henri-Matisse

Large Seated Nude, 1925

It was no accident that Matisse completed one of his finest and best known sculptures *(above)* during the period when he painted many of his best odalisques. He understood the female body as well as any man who ever lived, although he often distorted it in his art. And he achieved this knowledge at least in part through sculpture, which forces the artist to think in three dimensions and physically to *feel* the forms he is creating. In explaining how to draw, Matisse once told his students: "Translate the curves of the body as in sculpture. Look for their volume and fullness. The outlines should be enough. Speaking of a melon one uses both hands to express in one gesture its spherical shape. In the same way, two lines are sufficient to express one form."

In the voluptuous odalisque at the right, Matisse practices what he had preached to his students. The odalisque is round and full, her ovoid head, abstracted hand and elongated foot seem modeled from clay. Had the artist not simplified the forms in this way, giving the figure the curves and mass of a statue, she would have been lost against the ornate background. Wild arabesques crowd the rug and walls, practically smothering even a large mirror in a lavish baroque frame; a lush, leafy, potted plant, a patterned cushion, and a tempting bowl of oranges also compete for the viewer's attention. Yet the nude easily asserts herself. Only around the face did Matisse interrupt the busy movement of the background, smudging it slightly, to make her features stand out more clearly.

Decorative Figure on an Ornamental Background, 1927

The Painter and His Model, 1917

Matisse painted women quite differently in his Paris studio than he did in the Mediterranean light of the Riviera. The painting above of the artist with his model shows Matisse in a somber autumn Parisian mood. Both figures are almost featureless in the gloom of the bare studio: the baroque mirror behind the model seems like a tarnished ornament left over from happier times. But two years later, in Nice—where he spent more and more of his time from 1917 onward—Matisse painted the same scene again. In the bright southern light, his model is revealed as an ample beauty languishing among gay flowers in a chintz-covered overstuffed armchair. Everything speaks of ease and plenitude. Where the Paris study suggested that Matisse could not bear to dwell on details, here everything is delineated; the pattern of the rug, objects on tables, even the painter's gaily striped pajamas. Now the model has a face and the artist paints his own bespectacled profile clearly. The spirit of Nice has enhanced this odalisque as it does the magnificent one on the following pages. The first Matisse odalisque to enter a French museum, it was bought by the government in 1922.

The Artist and His Model, 1919

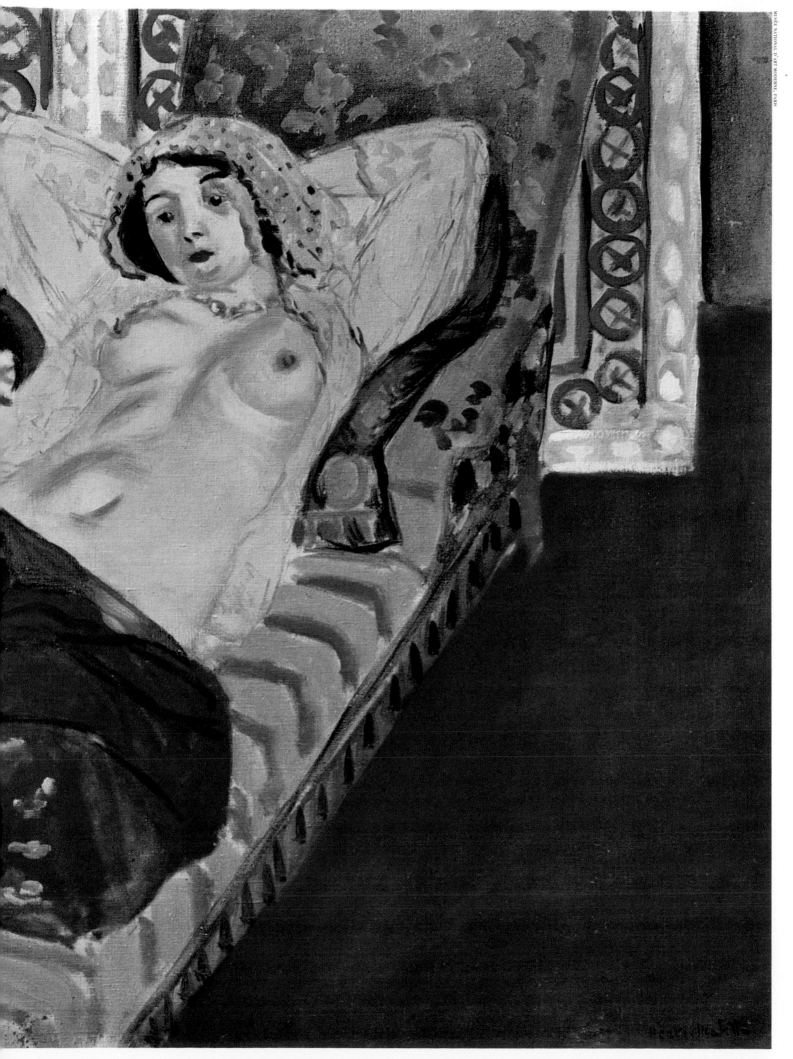

Odalisque in Red Trousers, 1922

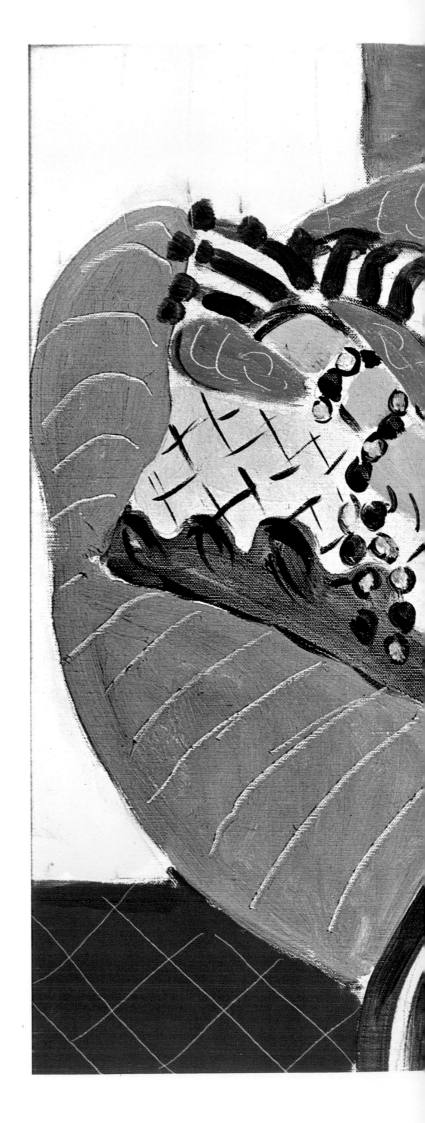

Pretty women in colorful costumes, the warm sun of southern France, the haunting indolence of the Moroccan odalisques—all these suggestions of pleasure bubbled up in Matisse's work for the rest of his life. In the 1930s he painted an aristocratic beauty, Princess Elena Galitzine, in exotic outfits. As an odalisque (*right*), the princess radiates a sophisticated elegance missing in many of the artist's earlier studies; her bold, handsome features and assured pose add to the luster. Matisse himself stressed the importance of his models. "My models," he said, "... are the principal theme in my work. I depend entirely on my model whom I observe at liberty, and then I decide on the pose that best suits her nature."

Matisse in his paintings created a world inhabited almost entirely by women. Occasionally he made a pencil portrait of a male friend, but in his painting life is seen in terms of femininity only. From the late 1930s on, he lived in a suite of rooms in the Hotel Regina on a sunny hilltop above the city of Nice: the sultan, in effect, of a perfectly ordered harem.

Henri Matisse 37

Odalisque with Striped Dress, 1937

116

VI

How to Paint a Masterpiece

The bright decorative effect of Matisse's work in the 1930s is seen in this portrait of his secretary Lydia Delektorskaya. Starting with a conventional pose on a graceful love seat, Matisse let the floor swoop up at the sides of the picture, flattened the space between the figure and the wall, and simplified all the shapes until the voluminous blue gown is complemented by a design of high-intensity red, black and yellow.

Lady in Blue, 1937

Matisse belonged to the generation of Frenchmen whose lives were clouded in childhood, in middle life and again in old age by the fact that France had an implacable enemy: Germany. He had grown up in a countryside permeated by the disasters of the Franco-Prussian War, and in 1914 he was sickened to see the whole thing happening all over again. Although Matisse was unfit for military service, his two sons would soon be of draft age and his younger colleagues—Braque, Derain and Vlaminck—were called up from the moment war was declared. Beyond that, one did not have to be a prophet to see that whatever the war's outcome an old idea of Europe was going down forever.

By 1914 Matisse was far too complete an artist to be deeply affected by external events. Still, he was sensitive to the changing times, and the war and its aftermath did to a degree influence his work. During the war his compositions became introspective, almost abstract, and when peace was restored they overflowed with delight in his physical environment. Typically, however, he continued to pursue his constant goal, the big picture, the masterpiece, and in 1927 he once again achieved it: *Decorative Figure on an Ornamental Background* was a painting that combined his love of pattern with his search for monumentality.

When the war began Matisse was 45. Although he could not fight he longed to make some contribution to his country's struggle. "What can I do?" he asked his old friend Marcel Sembat, now Minister of Public Works. "Go on painting good pictures," Sembat replied. And so, in the fall of 1914, Matisse once again went south to Collioure.

At Collioure he found an old friend, Marquet, and a new one, the gifted young Spanish painter Juan Gris, who had formerly been a neighbor of Picasso in Paris and who had been influenced by Picasso to try Cubism. Gris was a natural intellectual, a painter who made up his mind in advance what he wanted a picture to look like, then manipulated the visual facts to fit. Anything sloppy or accidental was abhorrent to him. "With a mind like mine," he once said, "how could I smudge a blue, or draw a line that wasn't straight?" Gris loved to talk, and it had been years since Matisse had had a companion of this sort. Not surprisingly, the gentle, unassertive Marquet was allowed to sink into contemplative silence while Matisse and Gris argued their heads off. "We talk painting relentlessly," Gris wrote a friend. "Marquet listens, but I think he's rather bored."

What was said on those occasions is unknown. But it is clear that Matisse was arguing out, trying to articulate, some of the problems and solutions inherent in painting a large, important picture. Once again, it seemed, he was quite consciously coming to grips with the job of creating a masterpiece. In 1897 this had led to *The Dinner Table*, in 1906 to *Joy of Life*, in 1909 and 1910 to *Dance* and *Music*, in 1911 to *The Painter's Family*. To each of these big paintings he had given all he had, but in each case what he had to give had been different. Now it was different again. For a long time, however, the nature of this difference was hidden from public view. The war had made painting almost a secret activity. There were no Salons at which to exhibit work, and no eager patrons dashing to Paris whenever there was word of something new. Many of Matisse's wartime paintings were packed away and were not seen in public until many years later.

Still, there were clues to what sort of paintings these might be. Shortly before the start of the war, Matisse had taken a studio in Paris at his old address on Quai St.-Michel—just for convenience' sake. Once again he looked upstream to Notre Dame, a subject that had always served him well. As a student he had painted the cathedral with all the careful attention to detail of an architectural draftsman. Later, when he was under the spell of Impressionism, he had gone all out to capture the fugitive effects of sunlight on it at every hour of the day. Subsequently he had painted it as old stone, as cotton candy, as melting ice cream. It seemed indeed that he had done almost everything with Notre Dame that it was possible to do. But in 1914, before leaving Paris, he did something new. He reduced the cathedral to a series of flesh-pink rectangles, turned the familiar outlines of the bridge and the quays into a network of thick black crisscrossing lines, indicated a cluster of trees with a patch of green and added another patch of greenish black to suggest the mat of evergreens hanging down over the embankment. It is hard to imagine a more abbreviated statement.

The following summer down at Collioure he produced another painting, no less drastic, called *The Open Window*. The title suggests one of the virtuoso pieces in which Matisse took such evident delight—the window with its shutters thrown open, the view of a southern sea and, in the foreground, the bowl of fresh-picked flowers. But *The Open Window* is not like that at all. The whole center of the picture is occupied by one huge black rectangle; on one side of it there is a weathered green shutter, on the other, an equally weathered blue wall. In conventional terms the picture is empty; there is nothing in it to look at.

Some critics have seen *The Open Window* as a symbol of the despair and emptiness to which the French people had been reduced by the prospect of an interminable war. Matisse was as much affected by this loss of moral energy as anyone. He complained to his friends of his ever greater difficulty in bringing his picture ideas to fruition as year after year he had to stand by, while the manhood of France was cut down. Yet *The Open Window* is not a pessimistic picture. On the contrary it is exciting and full of promise. Anything could be happening within this darkened rectangle or nothing could be happening at all. And is the rectangle a darkened room seen from outside, or a night landscape seen from within? It is as fascinating and mysterious as the dark recesses on Delphi where the oracle lay hidden.

The Open Window was a painting 40 years ahead of its time. Matisse in 1914 had done what American painters like Barnett Newman and Kenneth Noland are doing today. He had created a picture in which several bands of color interact upon one another so meaningfully as to make all other kinds of painting seem fussy and outdated. Several years before, Matisse had spoken of a wish to make an art that healed, as sunshine and high altitudes and a simplified existence were once thought to heal tuberculosis. *The Open Window* is that sort of picture: it works upon the vision as fresh air works upon the body, making one feel larger, freer, better.

Matisse could have gone on from this picture to invent a totally nonobjective art, but he was too typically French to push that far ahead of society. Besides, he truly loved to paint objects—flowers, pretty women, odd bits of furniture, the view from his window, the scrolled pattern of the music rack on his Pleyel piano. Also he genuinely enjoyed reworking the traditional themes of French art, and especially during the war he seemed to draw strength from these themes. In the spring of 1916, for example, when the Battle of Verdun was weakening France like some unquenchable hemorrhage, Matisse wrote a friend that he felt "good for nothing"; shutting himself up in his studio on Quai Saint-Michel he produced a series of little head-on portraits that go straight back to the eyeball-to-eyeball scrutiny of the people in the 16th Century portraits of Corneille de Lyon and François Clouet. Simultaneously, he painted several still lifes of a favorite pewter pot in which the robust modeling and the beautiful whites rival those in the still lifes of the 18th Century painter Chardin.

Today Matisse's wartime paintings look like votive offerings to the

Matisse came as close as he ever did to pure abstraction in these two pictures, painted within a few months of each other in the summer of 1914. *View of Notre Dame (left)* shows the twin towers of the Gothic cathedral ruthlessly simplified as stark rectangles looming over the Seine bridge and quays, which are represented by a few harsh lines. In *Open Window, Collioure (right)*, Matisse again paints a view through a window (or is it *of* a window?) but this time he reduced the elements—shutters, wall, window frame—to bold rectangles of flat color. Soon after he painted these innovative pictures, his style changed once again, never to return to such rigidly geometric abstraction.

gods of war, designed to persuade them not to interrupt the continuity of French life. While other French painters identified themselves with France by painting panoramas of munitions factories or portraits of the Unknown Soldier, Matisse expressed his patriotism by painting the France he knew best: his home, his family, his garden. Issy-les-Moulineaux's zigzag-patterned rugs, the scrolled balustrade outside its ground-floor windows, the curve of a chair arm, the look of the radiators, the dressing-table top scattered with brooches, the cylindrical bowl that held the goldfish—Matisse put them all into so many pictures that today Issy-les-Moulineaux seems almost as familiar as if one had lived there oneself. It is as if he wanted to give these mundane objects the permanence that comes with spiritual as well as material existence. Once known completely, through his pictures, they could never be completely destroyed.

In a paradoxical way, the war helped Matisse to move ahead to another stage in his art. There were no critics to bother him, no dealers and annual shows to think of, no frivolous visitors to take up his time, no colleagues to disturb his concentration. He had ample opportunity to pursue a goal that was never far from his mind, the creation of a fully accomplished, out-and-out masterpiece. Happily, he also had plenty of room in which to conduct the search. His garden at Issy still held the temporary studio, put up to accommodate his work on the Shchukin murals; he had a ground-floor studio in the house itself; and he had the studio in town, in his old quarters on Quai Saint-Michel. Making the most of this clear run, and despite continuing bouts with influenza that left him weak and giddy, Matisse moved ahead during 1916 and 1917 on a whole series of monumental canvases.

Unlike the small portraits and still lifes that apotheosized the familiar, these big paintings stretched the language of art in several directions at once. Most of them are flat paintings, without depth, and

Matisse and his equally sedate friend and neighbor Albert Marquet joined a lively crowd of younger painters in the Dutch artist Kees van Dongen's Paris studio at a costume party in 1913. Matisse, squatting on his heels in the right foreground, and Marquet, standing behind him, dressed up as hairy-chested wrestlers in long johns, striped shorts and bushy beards. The turbaned host and his wife are posed in the rear of the group, beneath the two middle Japanese lanterns.

their basic unit of construction, as in *The Open Window*, is a tall parallelogram of unbroken color. Matisse laid these tall panels in a frieze across his picture. The idea of sectioning off a painting with panels of flat color was not especially new. The Old Masters often set off what was happening in the foreground of their paintings by backing up the various elements with flat planes of color. But Matisse's colored panels are neither foreground nor background. They exist independently of the objects in the picture, and are the objects' equals.

In *The Open Window* the flat planes of color had formed a private, abstract world; there was nothing in the painting to tie it to any known place. But the big panel paintings that followed it included a wealth of identifiable detail. One of them is *The Piano Lesson*; it is obviously set in Matisse's own living room at Issy, and the pianist is his son Pierre. There is the familiar French window with its scrolled balustrade and view of the garden, the Pleyel piano with its music rack and metronome, and behind the piano, on the wall, a painting of Matisse's own painting, *Woman on a High Stool.*

It is especially easy to place *The Piano Lesson* because shortly afterward Matisse painted a straightforward, naturalistic picture of the same scene, *The Music Lesson.* Pierre Matisse remembers being called in from the garden to pose for it one hot summer's day in 1917: he and his brother Jean had been pelting each other with pears. Matisse asked Pierre to sit at the piano and placed his sister Marguerite beside him, to turn the pages. He put Jean to the left, in an armchair, and Madame Matisse in a rocking chair, out in the garden. On top of the piano he placed his violin, in its opened case, and beside it he placed a volume of Haydn's sonatas, positioning it so that the title ran vertically through the picture, to emphasize the sense of depth.

Matisse never made art correspond more closely to everyday experience than he did in this picture. *The Music Lesson* is a kind of well-turned, wary autobiography. Here is the well-kept suburban home with its scuffed but comfortable furniture, the well-behaved children reading or practicing under the watchful eye of their exemplary mother. All that is missing is a cross-stitched sampler on the wall. The same scene in the hands of less gifted artists was to become the standard commodity of French art in the 1920s and 1930s.

The Piano Lesson and *The Music Lesson* were very different sorts of pictures. One was literal and easy to read; the other was an abstract color study that looked haphazard but actually represented years of careful thought. Both pictures, however, derived from reality—they were both pictures of Matisse's own living room. But when Matisse left the house and padded across the lawn to his studio in the garden, he left that real world behind to work in the world of his imagination. There was nothing in the studio to anchor him to fact. It housed the dream world of *Dance* and *Music*, the two pictures he had painted for Shchukin in 1910. In 1916 and 1917, he entered that dream world again, this time in the context of his North African experiences.

French North Africa occupied a special place in the thoughts of French painters and writers. It stood for light and color, for the liber-

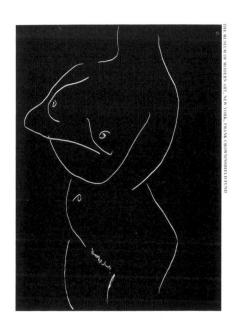

Among the prints Matisse executed in 1914-
1915, the one above, *Nude Torso, Arms
Folded*, is outstanding for its precise, spare
line. It is a monotype, a single print as unique
as a painting. It is made by covering a plate
with printer's ink or paint and scratching out
the design with a stylus before the plate is
pressed onto paper. In the printing process
the pattern is blurred and a second, identical
print cannot be made. Even the self-critical
Matisse was pleased with this creation of
elegant white lines on a black ground.

ation of the senses, for a lost paradise. French travelers there put aside
careworn identities and were reborn. The North Africans were a subject people, but they seemed to possess the secret to a dream existence,
a kind of life in which time did not matter and food was there for the asking and sex was taken for granted. Adventurous Frenchmen "went native" in North Africa without the slightest compunction.

Although Matisse was no adventurer, he did come away from North
Africa with very strong and exact impressions of the life there, and he
wanted to set them down without bothering too much with literal de-
scription. He had already recorded the actual North Africa in a series
of pictures done shortly after his two visits to Morocco in the winters
of 1912 and 1913. Now he wanted to paint his own private memory of
that experience. Two large paintings resulted: *Bathers by a River (page
90)* and *The Moroccans (page 90-91)*. *The Moroccans* was wall-size, 70
by 110 inches, and *Bathers by a River* was even larger, 103 by 154 inches. Both are tributes to a people who had learned to simplify life as Matisse was to simplify painting. Both are also grand, spare architectural
compositions in which Matisse took enormous liberties with the normal processes of pictorial representation.

It is easy to describe what these pictures contain. *Bathers by a River*
shows four girls, some tropical foliage and a snake. *The Moroccans*, a
scene of small-town life, shows a mosque, a balcony, a latticed pergola,
a house with shuttered windows, a pile of melons in a marketplace and
a group of crouching Moroccans wrapped in their burnooses. It is not
easy to describe how Matisse has taken all these things apart, simplified
and abstracted them, and turned them into symbols. *Bathers by a River*
and *The Moroccans* are not illustrations; they are monumental images.

Even today these two paintings are astonishing for the freedom and
daring of the manner in which Matisse played with reality. Yet the stark-
ly simple *Bathers* are not mere symbols; they are as hesitant and cranelike
as real women would be under similar circumstances. The landscape is
real too, although Matisse has reduced it to a dense growth of tart
green leaves; there is a sense of the nearness of water, of the sharp cutting edge of the leaves, of the abrupt contrasts of light and shade in the
semitropics. As for the little snake, raising his questing body and sharp-
pointed head from the bottom of the picture, he seems an impromptu af-
terthought. Yet he happens to be an essential part of the design. If he
were not there, the rest of the picture would pull away like a balloon
cut loose from its mooring.

In *The Moroccans*, Matisse was able to pack his picture with information
about how things looked by abandoning conventional perspective and
making the eye travel up, down and across all at the same time. He had always been interested in the way objects resembled one another,
particularly in the way the human body took on the appearance of everything from a cathedral to a piece of fruit. Moroccan men made this
point especially well, partly because their clothes were so expressive,
partly because they often sat motionless for hours on end. So *The Moroccans* is in one sense a study in form: it is about the roundness that
men and melons and mosques have in common. It is also about the spare-

ness and simplicity of Arab life, and the way that life shapes up into a well-proportioned spectacle—an experience usually denied to Americans and Europeans. Finally, it is about the making of a picture: how to take from a scene the forms that are needed, how to dispense with the ones that are not; how to end up with a picture that relates both to the scene, and to one's own private vision.

The strain of working at the top of his energies on pictures of three different kinds must have sometimes been unbearable, but Matisse never spoke of it. Painters in novels who work at such a pitch drop dead. But in real life—especially when the life is that of Henri Matisse—an inner voice always sounds a warning. In December 1916, Matisse heard the voice and made a decision that was to influence the whole future course of his career. He decided to take a rest, and travel south to see what winter was like in Nice. It suited him, and the following year he went back. From then on, Nice became increasingly the center of his working life.

Nice in those days was still relatively uncommercial. "When I first looked out the window and said to myself 'This is all mine, for as long as I like to have it,' " Matisse said many years later, "I simply couldn't believe my good fortune." The city had kept some of the quality of undiscovered paradise that Victorian watercolorists had stumbled on, but it also had something of the bustle and color of other great southern cities by the sea—of its near neighbor Genoa, for instance. Along the wide Promenade des Anglais the big waterfront hotels were perfect examples of seaside-playground architecture. In the old part of town the open markets were filled, day after day, with fennel and sea bass and oranges fresh from the tree. The light was not glarey and relentless, as it was in so many other parts of southern France, but subtle and endlessly varied. Waking up in a tall-ceilinged room overlooking the boat-filled harbor of the Baie des Anges was like waking up in a theater where the lights have just gone up, and the play is different every day.

Matisse, who was pushing 50, was very soon in greatly improved physical shape. He exercised regularly, particularly by rowing. He became an enthusiastic member of the Club Nautique, and could often be glimpsed pulling steadily out to sea, a square-built man in a single scull. During one nine-month period he went rowing no fewer than 154 times, and for this won the Club's medal—"for assiduity," as he put it. He also bought an automobile in a day when automobiles were a rarity, and taught himself to guide it down the middle of the road at a conservative speed. (When a friend asked him what he would do if he met a car coming in the opposite direction, Matisse said, "Well, in *that* case, I should bring my machine to a halt, get down, and sit by the side of the road until the other machine had passed.")

For five years Matisse passed every winter, from December to May, in one of the big sea-front hotels, and every day his routine was the same. At seven he would rise and make his way to a remote bathroom where, out of his fellow guests' hearing, he would practice the violin for two hours. (Matisse loved this instrument for its own sake—he never painted anything more tenderly than the sky-blue silk lining of its case—but he also had a favorite notion that if his eyesight should

The fierce, bearded Oriental warrior above is one of Matisse's drawings for his first venture with costume design. It was done for a 1920 production of *Le chant du rossignol*, a ballet with music by Stravinsky based on "The Nightingale's Song," one of Hans Christian Andersen's fairy tales. The Russian impresario Sergei Diaghilev persuaded Matisse to apply his art to the theater after Picasso had done so with brilliant success. The ballet was a failure, and some critics jeered at Matisse's delicate design and color, although they suit the exquisite story.

ever fail him, he could support his family by playing in the street.)

From nine to twelve Matisse would work at his easel, most often from a model, and after lunch he would either take a siesta or stroll past the Aleppo pines and the parasol pines in the Jardin Albert Premier, to one of the cafés on the Place Masséna. At four he would go back to work, and in the evening when the daylight was gone, he would close the shutters and put aside his brush, to draw some aspect of whatever had occupied him during the day. Continuity of effort was essential to him. He was tormented, for instance, when the local girls he recruited to be his models asked for a day off. And when the annual carnival season came around, he resigned himself to posing them so that they could watch the fun in the street below—instead of fidgeting.

The Nice paintings from the first were very special in character. To begin with they were much closer to the facts of actual vision than Matisse's other work. In Paris, he consistently abstracted and formalized what he saw; in Nice his eye, in effect, toured his hotel room and itemized every detail. There was also, in the Nice paintings, an unaccustomed sense of relaxation. The self-portrait he painted at Nice during his first winter there shows a country gentleman in a well-cut tweed suit, sitting at his easel, engaged in a task well within his powers: the picture has none of the strain and anguish of the self-portrait painted in 1906 at Collioure. For years Matisse's aim had been to change the future of painting, and the pictures that resulted had been intensely demanding. Now, suddenly, he had relaxed, and the art he set before the public was one of pure pleasure.

The public loved it. Even before the end of the war there was a new warmth in its response. In January 1918, when Matisse shared a show with Picasso at the Paul Guillaume Gallery, Apollinaire remarked, in the foreword to the catalog, that the beauty of the southern light seemed to have inspired Matisse to trust in the power and authenticity of his own instincts. People became convinced that a very pure and rare kind of happiness was to be got from ownership of a Matisse painting. In fact the Nice paintings came to stand for a certain idea of French civilization. This was life as it could be, ought to be, and better be—serene, ordered, delicious in every detail, and available to everyone.

The image, of course, wasn't quite true. Even in Nice reality did not consist of pretty women lying around naked, in bedrooms heaped high with flowers. Nor was there anything intrinsically delicious about the black umbrella hanging on Matisse's washstand. What looked simple and spontaneous was in fact the result of hard work, but the spirit behind the hard work was different. The difference is explained by two similar paintings, one done in Paris in 1917, the other done in Nice two years later. In the *Painter and his Model (page 110)*, painted in the studio on the Quai St.-Michel, Matisse analyzed and simplified his subject. He took it down to its bare bones. The room itself is divided squarely down the middle into a light area and a dark area, and both areas are plain to the point of austerity. The model has been reduced to an anonymous female figure sitting in a chair, and the artist himself, in the foreground, is an amorphous, bolsterlike shape; neither has any identity.

Matisse occupied a balconied top-story apartment in this building in Nice for 17 years. Although he fled the Côte d'Azur's burning, blinding sun in the summer, the apartment remained his home base from 1921 to 1938. The photograph above, taken during World War II, shows the yellow-washed building splotched with dark paint for camouflage against air raids.

In 1929 Matisse let his painting lie fallow, turning to sculpture and graphics; in a few months he had etched more than 120 plates. Like *Femme couchée au chien (Reclining Woman with Dog)* at left, these delicate etchings of women reflect the motifs he favored at the time. He posed his model, often with pet animals or goldfish, against an intricately patterned background and materials that set off her languorous charm. Working directly from the model before him he would scratch his drawing on the copper plate itself rather than sketch first on paper and then transfer his design to the plate.

In the Nice painting, *Artist and his Model (page 111)*, the conditions are reversed. The artist is clearly Matisse himself, sitting at his easel in striped pajamas, and the naked model is a desirable and highly individualized plaything. Where the Paris room was large and spare, this one is small and luxuriant. Except for the canvas in front of the artist, there is not an undecorated surface in sight. Curtains, wallpaper, tablecloth, cushions, two still lifes of flowers, and the tiled floor—every surface is broken and fragmented by pattern. The contrast with the severe parallelograms of the Paris picture is absolute.

Matisse was not playing with art in the Nice pictures, but he was in a sense playing with life. Like a sundial he was marking only the cloudless hours. The scenes he painted were devoid of strain, and his women took on the timeless languor of the harem women he had studied in North Africa (one of his favorite props, in fact, was a decorative, half-transparent harem screen that he brought back from Morocco). People, worn out by the war, wanted to believe that the world of these pictures was real. Within a decade the Nice paintings were selling for as much as $10,000 at auction—more than even the finest of the Matisse paintings had brought before 1914.

In the fall of 1921 Matisse decided to exchange his hotel-room existence for an apartment. A hotel room does not make an ideal studio, and Matisse was finding it tiresome to have to move out each May, when the hotels closed for the season. Besides he considered the rates, roughly $5 a day for each member of his family, rather high; Matisse was always careful about money. His new quarters were on the Place Charles-Félix in the old section of town, a part of Nice that had existed long before anyone thought of going to the south of France for pleasure. The apartment belonged to the American author Frank Harris, who had used it to write his amorous, near-pornographic autobiography, *My Life and Loves.* What Matisse thought of the Harris book is not on record, but he very much enjoyed the Harris apartment. It was on the top floor of a tall, ochre-washed building and looked out to sea across a two-storied, barrackslike structure called Les Ponchettes, past whose crumbling arches one got an occasional whiff of Nice's sister cities across the Mediterranean—of Tunis, perhaps, or Algiers.

Matisse's own building was Italianate in style, with an imposing staircase of solid marble and some unpretentious frescoes; many of its other inhabitants were singers from the nearby opera house. Close by was the Baroque church of St. François de Paule, and the fish and vegetable markets ran almost up to his front door. He took a liking to a restaurant across the way, Chez Albert, frequented by young advocates from the Nice law courts, and sometimes in the evenings he went off to the local art school, the École des Arts Décoratifs, run by one of his old classmates at Gustave Moreau's, Paul Audra. There he would draw from the cast as patiently as ever. He had a few artist friends not far away—Simon Bussy was at Roquebrune-Cap Martin and Pierre Bonnard was at Antibes—but for the most part Matisse led the life of a monk, a kind of life he had always wanted, with all the practicalities of life taken care of, and the day divided into an unvarying routine.

Matisse loved Nice and painted it with pleasure even on the days when the Promenade des Anglais was swept by hailstones and the Baie des Anges turned from blue to café-au-lait. But the greatest pictures of the Nice period are those of indoor scenes, in which there is a beautiful balance between the brilliance of the light outside and the filtered light within. Matisse was by this time on easy terms with the art of the past—even Cézanne, with whom he had wrestled so doggedly, was by now a friend rather than an antagonist—and many of the Nice paintings are variations on the themes of earlier French masters. There are echoes of Chardin and Manet in the Nice still lifes, of Ingres in the paintings of odalisques, of Delacroix in the imaginary harem scenes. Matisse did not so much copy these past masters as ask himself what they had been up to, and then feed the answer through his own sensibilities.

The Nice pictures were portraits of total fulfillment, serene in the way that Matisse had always wanted his pictures to be. Every part of each painting was as important as every other part; there were no areas of climax and no areas in which the touch became dry and mechanical. Although the things he chose to paint were things that always charm—freshly picked lemons, newly waxed furniture, the reflected glitter of a sunlit sea, women in never-before-worn summer frocks—the manner in which he painted them was equally charming. The paint was as beautiful as anything it described. Matisse once said that the surface of a picture "should carry *within itself* its complete significance." The Nice paintings illustrate what he meant—they make their point as paintings even before one has identified what they are about.

No earlier painter had ever quite done this. When in the Rococo period Boucher painted a pretty girl, naked or half naked, the prettiness of the girl got all his attention and the rest of the picture was just support. Chardin, who was incomparable at rendering "the shaggy velvet of the peach, the amber transparency of the white grape, the moist crimson of strawberries," nevertheless surrounded these superlative objects with other objects that were simply filled in. Delacroix, who like Matisse had visited North Africa and had been fascinated by its odalisques, set down his memories of these harem playthings in a series of portraits. Like Matisse, he fastened upon their provocative costume—the knee-length pantaloons, the silk jerkin slashed to the waist, the turban, the gold ornaments at wrist and throat—but unlike Matisse he painted them in traditional chiaroscuro. Not so Matisse. His odalisques play out the masquerade of their captivity in the full, even, saturated light of the Mediterranean.

The Nice paintings create a kind of toytown for adults, in which all the toys are new and none will ever get broken. Matisse went on adding and adding to their contents until every square inch of canvas was filled —piling pineapples upon an antique phonograph, putting real flowers against fake ones, even painting a small reflection of himself into a mirror hanging on a wall. They were a delight to paint and a delight to look at. To a Europe battered by war, they were even more than that: they contributed to Europe's spiritual convalescence. People who had forgotten what it was like to sit in the sun and have happy thoughts were persuaded that such a life was still possible. The idea of pleasure was reborn, and Matisse helped to bring it back to life.

This achievement would have been enough to satisfy most people, but not Matisse. Something was lacking in the Nice pictures that had been present in the earlier pictures: monumentality. Looking at them, one did not feel that the image before him was of something grander, stronger and more definitive than anything he himself could have imagined. The absence of this quality made Matisse restless, and in 1922, not by accident, he turned again to the art form which is by nature monumental: sculpture. The result, after three years of work, was *Seated Nude*, the largest of his sculptures since 1908. The pose for it was one that clearly obsessed him: a seated woman, leaning backward, her hands clasped over her head, one leg drawn up with its foot tucked under the other knee. He used it in a drawing in 1923, then repeated it in several lithographs and in 1924 put it into a painting, *Nude Seated on a Blue Cushion*. In the sculpture the figure rests in space, backed up by nothing but air; in the painting, the body's powerful curves are set off by the curves of the chair and cushion, and by the rectangular forms of brightly patterned wall hangings and carpets.

To make something monumental out of an actual, identifiable human body was not an easy thing to do. Matisse had to find a pose that flowed in one unbroken line from head to feet and back again, but at the same time he had to deal with the inconveniences of reality. It is one thing to imagine an impeccable line, and quite another to adjust it to the fact that breasts do not always fall in the right way, nor do the muscles of an upraised leg always bulge in the right place. The body may by nature be stiff and taut where, for the artist's purposes, it should be relaxed, and it may bunch up into ugly, unsculptural effects at precisely the point where the artist wished it to be pared and flattened. Art and life had somehow to be reconciled.

At such times Matisse habitually withdrew into his studio like Noah into his ark. The social amenities meant nothing to him. Calling on his old friend Marquet in Paris, he scarcely pretended to look at Marquet's new work before heading for the earlier Matisse nudes hanging on the wall. "Forgive me," he would say, "but I can't think of anything except what I'm doing myself." "I felt like a curate," Marquet later remarked, "when the bishop comes to call." For a time, in this period of searching, Matisse allowed life to dictate to art. The odalisques who occupy the center of a number of decorative interiors done in the early 1920s turn out to be, on close examination, not idealized playthings but middle-class Frenchwomen running slightly to fat, their faces are vacant and bloated looking, and they are none too stylish in the way they sit. Also—and this was new for Matisse, whose nudes were usually timeless—they clearly belong to the 1920s, from the way they wear their hair and pluck their eyebrows.

But once again, something got in the way of monumentality. The truthful sagging, the poignant flabbiness, pulled the painting down to earth. The result was interesting psychologically, but Matisse felt no obligation to explore the psychological predicament of middle-class Frenchwomen. That, to him, was the function of the novel. Besides, it would upset the pictorial balance to give the human body a weight of feeling that could not be shared by the other parts of the picture—the carpet, the flowers, the furniture—and to Matisse that balance was essential. Also, in Matisse's view, any emphasis on the fleeting aspect of human beauty was out of place: to him flesh tainted by age was as welcome as a pear half-eaten by wasps.

Actually, in his quest for monumentality, Matisse did not need to look any further than the walls of his own home, where there hung a much-worn 18th Century portrait of a grand, impassive Tibetan lama, and nearby, carefully protected by glass, a fragile but still beautiful 16th Century Persian carpet. In the immobility of the lama and the insistent arabesque pattern of the carpet, Matisse found the inspiration for the big painting that finally exorcised his demon: *Decorative Figure on an Ornamental Background (page 109).* The preliminary drawings for this painting show the model slumping languidly against the wall, but in the painting itself, completed in 1927, he altered her position: her body is square-cut and upright, with a helmetlike head and small stylized breasts that come not from life but from Matisse's own sculptured *Seated Nude.*

Decorative Figure on an Ornamental Background is the culmination of

Matisse usually turned to sculpture as a three-dimensional exercise that refreshed him from his struggle with the two dimensions of painting. In one instance, however, he brought the two arts together as he experimented, over more than 20 years, with a series of low-relief sculptures of a female back. Four reliefs—life-size or larger—were completed between the years 1909 and 1929. They constitute a unique one-man, one-subject history of modern art. Beginning with a careful, almost naturalistic study that is still rooted in the 19th Century, Matisse progressively simplified until finally the back is reduced to two tall columns divided by a third, a thick tress of hair. The trend is clearly away from an imitation of nature and toward a goal that Matisse had in mind in sculpture as much as in painting: to make an equivalent for the human body that would be more "true to life" than any painstaking representation of everyday visual experience —more accurate and meaningful for being a pure product of the artist's creativity.

everything that occupied Matisse's attention during the Nice period: pattern, monumentality, the beauty of ordinary objects, the sensuality of the naked female body. Its central figure is powerful enough to hold its own against a background patterned more insistently than anything since the 1909 *Harmony in Red*. There is an arabesque patterned wallpaper, a Persian-print carpet, a flowered cushion, a figured flowerpot, a bowl of fruit and a gilded Baroque mirror—and all of it seems to be talking at the top of its lungs. Matisse had to cheat a little bit to bring it all off —but only a little. The pressure of the patterning behind the model's head is toned down ever so slightly, and a drapery over the lower part of her body isolates it from its immediate surroundings. The picture is one of the most aggressively successful he ever painted, and having completed it, his investigations temporarily came to a halt.

Matisse is one of the great examples of what the French refer to as *la clarté française*, by which they mean not just "clarity" but clear-mindedness: the ability to know exactly what one is doing and why. By 1927 he had been working in Nice for just on 10 years. He was living, by his own wish, a life of dedicated retirement and he had made himself a new reputation as the poet laureate of a carefree, monied society that liked nothing better than seeing the Good Life made visible in Matisse's paintings. But there was something facile about this success that vexed Matisse. Too many of his great paintings were unknown to this new public. In 1927, as if to set the record straight, he brought some of them out. He sent *The Moroccans* to New York for a show arranged by his son Pierre at the Valentine Dudensing Gallery (Pierre had gone to the United States in 1924 and was making a name for himself as an art dealer). Later that year Matisse shipped *The Piano Lesson* and *Bathers by a River* to an exhibition in Paris.

During that same year, the Carnegie International Exhibition in Pittsburgh confirmed Matisse's American reputation by awarding him its first prize for *Fruits and Flowers*, a typically sumptuous still life from the Nice period. But Matisse, instead of capitalizing on this success, practically gave up painting. In 1929, for instance, he put his main efforts into well over 100 etchings, and into a bronze bas-relief, *The Back* (the fourth in a series of studies of the female back, begun in 1909, in each of which he had taken increasingly greater liberties with anatomy). It was as if Matisse, listening to the voice of *la clarté française*, had decided to let painting lie dormant until something happened to give it a new direction.

Suddenly, in 1930, that impetus was provided. The Carnegie International invited him to come to Pittsburgh to serve on the jury of its current show. Normally Matisse would not have considered closing up his studio to travel abroad and look at other people's paintings. But the invitation seemed to coincide with the stirring of a long-dormant wish: for years Matisse had wanted to see the South Seas. Why not, he thought, do both? And so he set off, first for the South Seas by way of New York—to visit his son Pierre—and then three months later for Pittsburgh to act as a Carnegie juror. From that decision came others, fundamental to the rest of his painting career.

Dance II, 1932-1933

The Struggle
for Simplicity

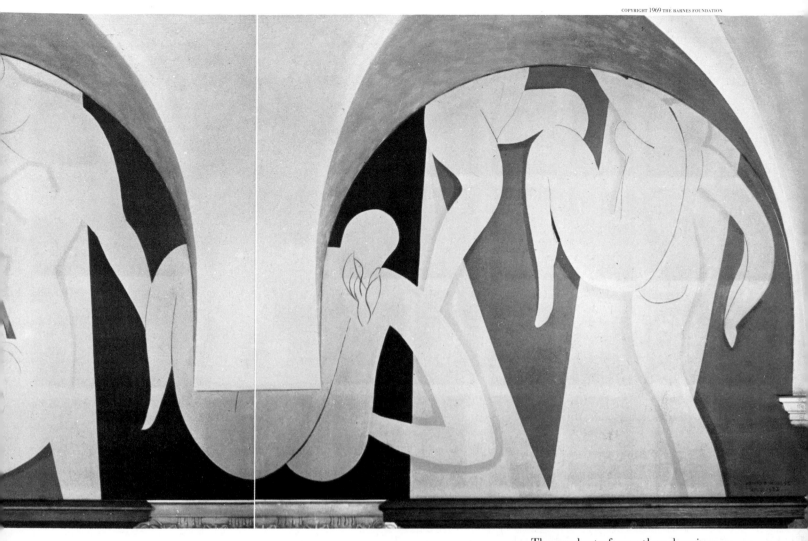

The product of countless drawings
and color sketches, the final
version of the Barnes mural,
Dance, shows the clean, stylistic
refinement of Matisse's mature art.

In 1930, Matisse, restless with the rigid schedule of
work he had imposed on himself for almost three decades,
threw off his well-ordered life and left France. He traveled
first to the United States, then to Tahiti to see for himself
the light—and the islands—that had captivated Gauguin.
The trip revived him and upon his return to Nice a year
later he undertook an immensely exacting project that
once again engaged his obsessive need to simplify painting.
The project was a gigantic and complicated mural *(above)*
for Dr. Albert Barnes of Merion, Pennsylvania. In it and the
paintings that followed, Matisse refined and distilled his art;
he made many versions of some of these works, and they
stand today as records that show step by step how he reduced
his painting to its simplest and purest state.

Matisse painted the Barnes mural not once but twice. The fate of the first might have broken the spirit—and the heart—of a lesser artist. The mural, commissioned in 1930, was to fit into three large arches high above the floor of the main room of the mansion housing Barnes's collection. Matisse decided that the theme of the mural would be the *Dance*, which he had used in an earlier commission done for the Moscow home of Sergei Shchukin *(pages 86-87)*. His early color sketches of the 11½-by-42-foot picture *(right)* are also reminiscent of the Shchukin work, with their roughhewn dancing maidens and raw colors. But in the finished version of the first

mural *(at right, below)*, Matisse refined the painting; the figures are cleanly drawn, the colors reserved.

After more than a year's work and anguish, Matisse sent the completed painting to Dr. Barnes for installation. There the sickening truth was discovered—the mural was five feet too short to fit the arches it had been ordered for. Resolutely, Matisse began again. About six months later, he emerged with an even more stylized result *(preceding page)*. The first version of the mural was not wasted, however. The Musée d'Art Moderne de la Ville de Paris purchased it in 1937. In 1968 it was shown *(above)* at a huge Matisse retrospective in London.

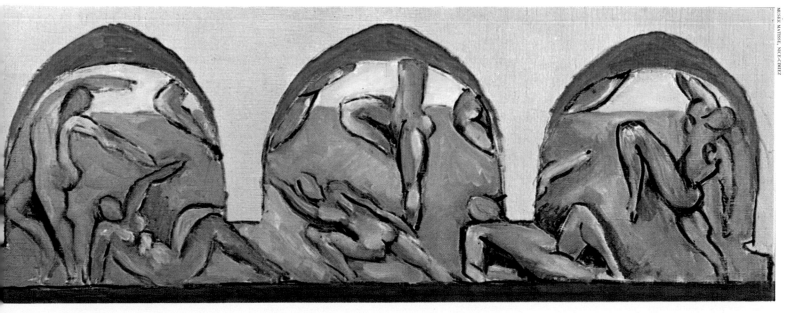

Dance I (preliminary sketch)

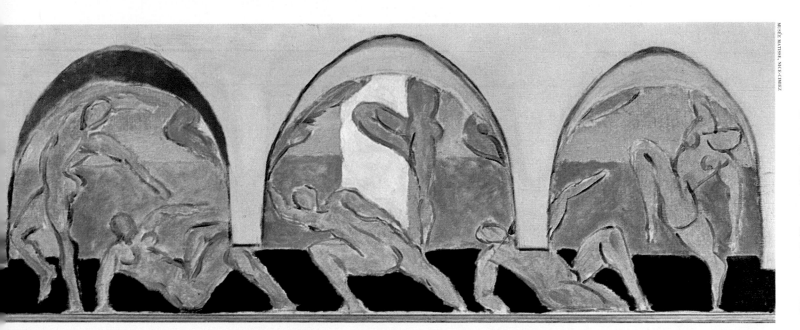

Dance I (preliminary sketch)

Dance 1, 1931-1932

133

1 2 3

9 10 11

17 18 19

20 21 22

Matisse left posterity a fascinating insight into his method of working when he had a series of black-and-white photographs taken of each of the 22 versions of his painting *Pink Nude*. His first study was completed on May 3, 1935 (1), his last was done by October 30. The numbered photographs above trace his struggle to produce a masterpiece. The *Pink Nude* begins as a portrait of a voluptuous girl on a sofa, the corner of the room providing a sense of traditional perspective. Searching for greater effect, Matisse flattens the painting by enlarging the girl's limbs and finally removing the room's corner (6). By the ninth version, the background is completely flat and the figure has been moved so far forward that both feet and an elbow run off the canvas. After a series of stretchings and alterations, the body totally dominates the picture (16). From this extreme, Matisse retracts the limbs, rounds the elbows and knees, and lessens the tension of the torso, softening it (18-20). Then the head is raised again (21), the left leg is tucked tighter to the body and the artist calls the work finished (*22 and right*).

5 6 7 8

13 14 15 16

Pink Nude, 1935

Red Still Life with Magnolia, 1941

Matisse's genius for organizing a picture was fundamental to his search for simplification. Even after the serious illness of 1940-1941, which left him weakened and often confined to his bed, his disciplined approach to composition held firm. One of his favorite still lifes completed at this time *(left)* has been compared with the tautly balanced Romanesque altarpieces that Matisse certainly knew in the churches and museums of southwestern France. In those religious works, Christ or the Madonna is placed at the center while four saints occupy the corners to add balance and strength. In the picture at left, a vase of leaves with one flower is the focal point; a platter with a handle provides a halolike background that also unifies the pitcher, the vase, the plant and the shell in the corners with the centerpiece. The sense of harmony here is so perfect that the removal of one of the objects would cause the entire composition to collapse.

Some of the objects in this painting, as well as some in *Tabac Royal (following pages)*, reflect Matisse's attachment to familiar accessories of his daily life. The pewter jug and the sea shell at left, the lute and the crockery jar labeled "Tabac Royal" on the next pages, were used by Matisse again and again. *Tabac Royal* is the fourth of a series of paintings completed by him in 1942-1943. They are all elaborate testimonies to his ability to find inspiration in the simplest things. Late in his life Matisse confided, "I have worked for years in order that people might say, 'It seems so easy to do.'"

137

Tabac Royal, 1943

VII

A Mural
for Dr. Barnes

Painted when Matisse was almost
80 years old, this portrait of the
interior of his studio is his last
great oil painting. Unified with a
vibrant red, the scene is bright with
the artist's sense of humor; beside
one of Matisse's own paintings
(upper right) the view through an
open window appears as flat as if it,
too, were painted; beneath the
table in the lower right a calico cat
is chased by a dog, both as abstract
as patterns on a carpet.

Large Red Interior, 1948

In 1930, when Matisse decided to go ahead with his idea of a trip to
New York and the South Seas, his career had reached a critical point.
For years he had been in effect walled up in his studio. He seldom saw
other painters and had almost no contact with the people who admired
and bought his paintings. Even his domestic life was solitary. Madame
Matisse was unwell and kept to her room for months on end, and the
three children were all out in the world. With nothing new to engage
his mind, his output of paintings had eased almost to a halt. True, he
was not idle; etchings, drypoints, lithographs and sculptures took the
place of the paintings. But there was no concealing the fact that he needed a change of scene. Methodical in all things, he chose to make that
change as radical as possible by taking in, within the space of a few
months, experiences as opposite to each other as New York City and
Tahiti.

Matisse loved New York from the start, so much so that he was tempted, he said, to cancel the rest of his trip and take a New York studio.
The change of light, the change of scale, the change of attitude in
every department of life were just what he needed. At a time when
most cultivated Europeans thought of the United States as a mechanized
Barbary, and of Americans as people who bought art but could not produce it, Matisse took a longer view. Without committing himself on
the current state of art in America, he implied that great things were in
store. To an interviewer from the *New York Times*, he observed that
every art was the logical result of its surroundings: "The gray skies of
Holland are reflected in Dutch paintings, just as the sunshine is reflected in Italian surroundings." In addition, said Matisse, "the thoughts
of the people as well as their activities all have their influence on the
paintings which their painters produce."

Pausing to wipe his thick spectacles with a light-brown silk hand-
kerchief that harmonized with his ginger-brown suit, Matisse went on
to speak of the special qualities of New York. He mentioned the look of
the city as one sailed into the harbor, and the view from the top of the
Woolworth Building, one of the world's first skyscrapers. "This is a dif-

ferent civilization from the one we have in Europe," he said. "No one can grasp the majestic grandeur of New York until he has actually seen it. I have seen it at the movies a thousand times, but its vastness is beyond all comprehension. . . . Compare all this with what existed fifty or a hundred years ago, and you will understand why such an apparently radical change has come over painting."

Much as he was captivated by New York, however, Matisse was not one to change a schedule. After a visit of only two or three days, he left for Polynesia, crossing the United States to San Francisco and embarking there for Tahiti. What took him to the South Seas was not a commonplace interest in the exotic; still less was it the disgust with Western civilization that had prompted Gauguin to go into exile. Matisse dreamed of finding a light stronger and more benign than any he had heretofore known; he hoped to find it in the South Seas, and he planned to give Tahiti three months in which to take effect. But it is not always easy to adapt to the reality of a place long dreamed of. Temperamentally the South Seas did not suit him at all. Matisse was a natural worrier who thrived on constructive anxiety, and in Tahiti worry was unknown. All the Europeans he met were bored, while the Tahitians seemed to him to be lacking in the moral dimension that comes from measuring the thing done against what might have been done.

At first he did not even think Tahiti beautiful. "I was dumfounded," he said, "though unconsciously I was building up a new store of images." The light, he saw, was totally different from the silvery, refined light in Nice: Matisse felt as if he were looking into the far depths of an immense goblet of gold. The sounds were different too: the irregular pounding of the waves on the reef mixed with the silken rustle of the trade winds in the tops of the coconut palms. Tahiti also confirmed his lifelong conviction that colors only achieve their identity in relation to one another. Looking at the fruits, foliage and flowers against the blue Tahitian sky, he saw how intense that relationship could be. Swimming in the lagoon—an activity that occupied a good half of his time—he

When pre-World War I Europeans found themselves living because of duty—or dereliction—in the more remote corners of the world, they usually tried to create "a bit of home" in their exotic surroundings. This Victorian rocker that Matisse sketched in Tahiti during his three-month visit in 1930 was apparently a relic of that colonial impulse—just as Matisse's desire to draw it may have reflected his own feeling of strangeness on that alien island; it was one of only a very few pieces of work he did during his entire stay.

noted how the color of the coral was set off by the black of the sea cucumbers, and how the sunlight shining through the water turned the bottom of the lagoon the color of absinthe.

Some painters would come back from such a visit with a stack of canvases. Matisse was not that sort of painter. What he wanted from Tahiti was a repertory of images to use later on. Although he filled page after page of his sketchbook with rough notes on what he saw, it was years before he made direct use of them. For a long time, in fact, it seemed that the one product of his stay in the South Seas was a pen-and-ink drawing, published in the magazine *Cahiers d'Art* in 1936, of an elaborately curlicued Victorian rocking chair in his Tahitian hotel room. Not until the last glorious phase of his career, in the 1950s, did his work reflect the colors and forms of the land and sea life he had seen during his stay in Tahiti.

In October 1930, Matisse returned to the United States to fulfill his duties as juryman for the 29th Carnegie International, a duty he shared with five other painters, the Austrian Karl Sterrer, the Englishman Glyn Philpot, two Americans, Bernard Karfiol and Ross Moffett, and a Canadian, Horatio Walker. From a field of 99 American painters and 137 Europeans, the prize went to Picasso for a severe, classical portrait of Madame Picasso. Matisse did not linger in Pittsburgh but returned almost immediately to New York. Reporters, catching up with him there, tried to draw him out, but he refused any but the most general questions. He did say, however, that he disliked Tahiti as a place to live, and could never work there—"I am no Gauguin"—but that he still very much admired New York and the United States. "American artists should not be ashamed of their own country," he said. "It is magnificent. Why do American painters go abroad when they have scenes of such varied beauty at home?"

From New York he made a quick trip south to see the two great Matisse collections in America, the Cone collection in Baltimore and the Barnes collection in suburban Philadelphia. In Baltimore he stayed with Miss Etta Cone (whose sister Dr. Claribel had just died), and Baltimore made much of him. But the visit that mattered most to him in terms of the future was his brief and formal call on Dr. Albert Barnes, the patent-medicine millionaire art collector in Merion, Pennsylvania. Dr. Barnes had begun buying Matisse's work shortly after seeing examples of it at the Steins' apartment in Paris, around 1914. He had gone on buying throughout the 1920s, with the result that his Matisse holdings were now the largest in America. Barnes was a difficult man with a brutish manner and a positive mania for man-to-man controversy. Nevertheless he could hardly have put his enormous fortune to better use. In its coverage of French art in the era bounded by Renoir, Cézanne, Seurat, Picasso and Matisse, the Barnes collection is unlikely ever to be equaled.

The Barnes Foundation, a building adjacent to Barnes' home, looks very much the same today as it did in 1930 when Matisse walked through its modest front door. What confronted him was—and still is—an amazing sight. He found himself in a galleried entrance hall, two stories high, on whose walls were his own *Riffian* of 1913 (purchased by Barnes from its original owner, the Danish collector Tetzen Lund); Seurat's *Les Poseuses*, a painting Matisse had not seen for 30 years; a large *Composition* of 1906 by Picasso; and one of the grandest of Cézanne's series of *Card Players* paintings. These were only a few of the major paintings that greeted Matisse as he continued his tour. On the landing of the staircase to the upper floor, for instance, he came upon his own *Joy of Life*, which had been sold by the Steins to Tetzen Lund, and by Lund to Dr. Barnes.

Matisse barely had time to take all this in when Barnes suddenly seized his arm and announced that he had made up his mind: Matisse must decorate the empty space above the French doors in the entrance hall—a space 11 feet high and 47 feet long. The doctor's appeal came as a surprise to Matisse, and he was not a man who liked surprises. Nor was he the type to be moved by such appeals. But Barnes was not like Matisse's other American patrons, the supercivilized Steins and Cones; he had a reputation for being a domineering and boorish man, and he insisted. In fact, he was so determined to win Matisse over that he very nearly caused him to miss a prearranged lunch date. When Matisse's escort to the lunch called at the Foundation to pick him up, he found the door locked and had to enter the building through an open coal chute.

Matisse was genuinely impressed by the beauty of the Barnes collection and by the discrimination with which it had been brought together. This, more than the doctor's powers of persuasion, finally convinced him to accept the Barnes commission. In retrospect, that acceptance seems fated to have happened. The commission came at a time when Matisse was disenchanted with easel painting and offered him an opportunity to work on an entirely different scale. It also came at a time when commissions from American patrons were rare, especially commissions for projects that were meant to be in effect integral parts of a building. Although he did not answer Dr. Barnes immediately, he continued to think about his proposal when he got back to France. More and more the commission seemed to be the "real right thing." In January 1931 he sent Dr. Barnes an unequivocal "yes," rented a deserted film studio in Nice, and got down to work.

Matisse saw in Barnes the good side of what some people took to be sheer perversity: the strict rules and regulations that he had established for the use of the Barnes Foundation. Barnes considered the Foundation to be a place for the serious study of art, and he was very selective about visitors. To see his pictures was a privilege, and the privilege had to be lived up to. Something in the singlemindedness of Barnes spoke to the singlemindedness in Matisse. For a patron who felt so strongly about art he would create something new, something he had never tried before. The United States had no dearth of great art by European painters, but it did not have a great European work of art that had been specially commissioned. Spurred on by Dr. Barnes, Matisse was determined to put this right.

The space to be filled consisted of three adjoining arched areas. Matisse could have treated them as three self-contained units. If he had,

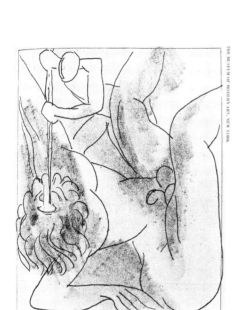

Matisse never portrayed physical agony until around 1935, when he agreed to etch illustrations, including some scenes of violence, for a new edition of James Joyce's epic novel *Ulysses* by the Limited Editions Club of New York. Painstaking as always, he searched art of the past for guidance. Among the works of a 15th Century Florentine painter and sculptor, Antonio Pollaiuolo, he found a small panel showing Hercules crushing the life out of the giant wrestler, Antaeus. He then adapted, modified and changed Pollaiuolo's upright Antaeus until it became the prone Matisse figure above.

the work would have seemed to be an additional row of easel paintings above those already on the wall. But the existing paintings were too great to brook this sort of interference, and the spaces that Matisse had to fill were too far above eye level for such a treatment to register effectively. Instead, Matisse decided to let the design flow across the top of the room in one unbroken horizontal movement that would complement the paintings below rather than attempt to rival them. The picture would be a thing more to sense than to look at—"One will *feel* my picture rather than see it," said Matisse; it would operate, he hoped, on the middle ground between painting and architecture, be "the equivalent of stone or cement."

In the great pictures on the wall below, the dominant theme was immobility. Cézanne's card players, silently studying their hands, looked as though their game would never get moving again. Seurat's naked models seemed locked in their poses for all eternity. Matisse's own seated *Riffian*, wrapped in his Berber cloak, stared fixedly out into space. To offset this concentrated stillness, Matisse decided to fill his mural with strenuous action. Once again he returned to a theme that had served him well several times in the past, the dance. But this time his dancing figures were engaged in superhuman exertions. They sprang high in the air, leaped and kicked, pounced upon one another, fell backwards and then collected themselves as if for another round of violent motion.

In Matisse's first sketches for the mural, the composition turned on one particular figure, a dancer just to the right of the center, in the middle panel. In a world of tumbling, spinning figures, she stood poised on one leg, as firm as a column on the Parthenon. Before long, however, Matisse discarded her—doubtless because her vertical stance interrupted the dynamic thrust of the composition from right to left, a thrust that began with a high-kicking figure on the extreme right and swept across to a leaping figure on the extreme left, whose leap takes her half out of the picture.

B y 1931 Matisse had worked out the final form of his composition, and in doing so had employed a drawing technique that was to be of singular importance to him later in his career. Habitually he drew his compositions full size, but he was accustomed to working in a scale that was comfortable to the human hand and arm—a scale small enough to allow him to cover a sheet of paper from end to end in a single sweep of his arm. For the larger Barnes mural, this was impossible. To approximate the free-running line of a normal-size drawing Matisse fastened a charcoal point to a six-foot pole and, standing before a huge sheet of paper tacked to his studio wall, outlined his figures. They were giant figures, and he emphasized their proportions by drawing them so that no figure was seen complete. In every case some part of the body—a head, the feet, even an entire torso—appeared to have been carried beyond the picture by the sheer force of the dancer's energy.

The final drafts of the Barnes mural showed Matisse to be, more than ever, a man bent on simplifying painting. In the first versions of the mural, the dancers are modeled as carefully as they would have been in a drawing by an Old Master: the bodies are three-dimensional

In the late 1930s, 26 eminent artists joined Matisse in accepting a commission from Steuben Glass, the American crystalware firm, to design decorations for a special collection. Matisse actually triggered the whole project; in 1937, after seeing a piece of engraved crystal, he had stunned a Steuben official, John M. Gates, by expressing interest in designing something for him. Matisse's contribution was a satyr playing double pipes. Made into an engraving by Steuben artisans, his free-flowing sketch framed in vine leaves *(top)*, became the Neo-Classic vase above.

and there is a certain amount of characterization. But gradually he flattened and simplified the figures, and he shifted the emphasis from the powerfully knotted and straining muscles to the bodies' pure outlines. From his vast knowledge of art history, Matisse was recalling the anatomical drawings of a 15th Century Italian, Antonio Pollaiuolo, and the spikey, incised figures on the black vases of ancient Greek potters.

To Matisse's close friends, it was clear that work on the Barnes mural was a tremendous strain. Ordinarily he came to call Sunday afternoons, driving up in his chauffeured American car; upon arriving he would seat himself in courtly fashion and entertain the assembled guests with anecdotes and stories. Matisse, when he felt like it, could be delightful company, and he possessed a gift for mimicry that impressed even the most exacting audiences (in fact, he would have made a good character actor, and was pleased to be told so). During his preoccupation with the Barnes mural, however, these gifts vanished from view. If he came to call at all, he would sit silent, visibly perturbed by the magnitude of his current task. He suffered as much as any beginning painter —more, perhaps—from the fear that all might not go well. At times he even cabled his friends for help: "Decoration in terrible state, composition completely out of hand in despair light suitable this afternoon for God's sake come at once Matisse," read one frantic appeal.

When Matisse, after months of preparation, finally set down his fully realized design, he did so all at one go. "It was inside me," he said, "like a rhythm that carried me along." But his satisfaction was short lived, for he ran headlong into a new problem: color. He had made many color sketches, most of them only a few inches wide. In one the bodies were tan and yellow on an ochre ground; in another, gray on white; a third showed them pale blue on greenish yellow; a fourth, gray-blue on a background of pink, black and ultramarine panels. None was right, but Matisse went on trying. The trouble was that large areas of color often take on a life of their own, altering the composition in ways that are unintended. And when he came to color his completed design, he found that his beautifully assured arrangement of forms had to be changed. "To arrive at something that was alive and singing I had to grope my way, modifying all the time...."

Because it was impractical to make these modifications in paint, Matisse hit upon the idea of cutting his tentative shapes from colored paper, which could be moved about easily and tacked on the wall. Before long the rare visitor who was permitted to enter the studio found Matisse standing in a welter of colored papers while working on a mural that was literally in pieces, pinned together on the wall. One by one, the problems dropped away. The figures were reduced to flat stone-gray shapes set against geometrical areas of color—pink, pale blue, black. The number of dancers was reduced to six, one of whom has leaped so high that she is almost lost to view while two others have momentarily dropped to the ground to watch their companions. As an evocation of pure physical high spirits it could hardly have been surpassed, and Matisse must have felt that he had discharged his obligation in the best French tradition of conscientious craftsmanship.

And so he had, except for one small flaw: he had gotten the measurements wrong. The mural was almost two yards too short. What Matisse said when he discovered the error has never been recorded. Some artists would have remedied the mistake by getting an assistant to calculate how much the design needed to be changed in order to fill the space —and then would have produced a second version that was essentially a modification of the first. But not Matisse. For him the corrected dimensions represented a fundamentally different design problem, and so he put aside a year's work and started all over again. After another nine months, a second mural emerged, unlike the first one in design and totally different in feeling. (The original mural was eventually purchased by the Musée d'Art Moderne de la Ville de Paris.)

The amiable galumphing dance of version I became in version II a mimed combat in which the dancers could very well have been fighting for their lives. The flow of energy, which in version I moved from right to left and went straight on out of the picture, in version II is turned around and sent bowling back again. In the side panels this movement runs upward and across, but in the center panel it turns downward sharply and spins round and round, counterclockwise, seemingly until the end of time. As for the two recumbent figures at the base of the mural, these became in version II less like resting dancers than majestic umpires —great, calm, monumental figures who are there to see fair play done but do not intend to exhaust themselves in the doing of it.

In May 1933, when the second version of the mural was finally finished, Matisse accompanied it to the United States to see how it suited the Foundation. Both he and Dr. Barnes were delighted. Matisse had wanted to avoid adding just one more painting to the collection, and he had succeeded. "As soon as I saw the decoration in place," he wrote, "I felt that it was detached absolutely from myself, and that it took on a meaning quite different from what it had had in my studio, when it was only a painted canvas. There in the Barnes Foundation it became a rigid thing, heavy as stone, and one that seemed to have been spontaneously created at the same time as the building. . . ." As for Dr. Barnes, he thought the mural the crown of his collection, "like the rose window of a cathedral."

The Barnes mural was a personal triumph for Matisse, but it was also a triumph for a way of working that is recognized as quintessentially French. Ever since Descartes had published his *Discourse on Method* in the 17th Century, Frenchmen had taken it for granted that any problem could be solved by anyone with "a healthy and attentive mind." All one had to do was break the problem down into its component parts. Matisse had been doing just this for many years; on the Barnes mural he happened to do it on a uniquely large scale.

The same method was also serving him well on a problem at the opposite end of the design scale. In 1930 he accepted an invitation from the Swiss publisher Albert Skira to illustrate a book of poems by the 19th Century French poet Stéphane Mallarmé. While the Barnes mural absorbed him during the winter in the south, he gave most of his attention in Paris in the summer to the Skira commission. Once again he

Informality and elegance balance each other in the cluster of figures that Matisse composed as a decoration over the fireplace in an apartment owned by one of the Rockefeller family in New York. The opposing curves of the two seated girls in the upper portion give the design much of its flowing grace; a note of gaiety appears in the lines of the singing girl in the lower portion, who seems to use the fireplace frame as a prop for her music. Surrounded by dark brown paneling, the composition glows with color. Matisse completed it in about three weeks in 1938.

broke down the problem into its component parts: the character of the poems themselves, the calligraphic style of the type from which the poems would be printed, and the hair-thin line made by the sapphire point of the etching needle.

Mallarmé's delicate poems are among the most famous in modern French literature and Matisse met the challenge head-on. The illustrations *(pages 154-155)* are all drawn in a line so fine that, as Matisse himself said, "the paper is left almost as white as it was before I went to work." He did not see the book as an album of pictures with verses alongside, but as a true and complete partnership between himself and the poet. "The two facing pages, the light one and the dark one," he said, "are like the white ball and the black one that a juggler plays with. They are completely unalike, and the point of the juggler's art is that he makes the spectator see harmony where none existed before."

The harmony achieved by Matisse in his work was soon to be lost to him in his private life. Europe from the mid-1930s onward was a doomed continent. For any sensitive person the only question was not whether war would come, but how soon. Matisse was acutely aware of this as a man—but he was also aware of it as an artist. One by one, his pictures were condemned as decadent and removed by the Nazis from the walls of German museums. In addition the former harmony of his life was interrupted by ill health and by his grief over his separation from Madame Matisse, a separation that by 1939 was all but final, although it was never legalized. French law would have required them to divide their possessions in half. For Matisse, this would have meant giving up half the contents of his studio, the work of many years.

Astonishingly, in these circumstances, Matisse not only kept going but actually broke new ground. In 1937, at the request of the American manufacturer of fine crystal, Steuben Glass, he designed a decorative motif for a vase. In 1938 he became involved in theatrical design, producing the sets and costumes for Leonide Massine's ballet, *Rouge et Noir*, danced by the Ballet Russe de Monte Carlo to music by Dmitri Shostakovitch. In less than three weeks in December 1938, he pushed through the design for an over-mantel decoration for the New York apartment of one of the Rockefellers.

Concurrently Matisse began, as it were, to clear the decks for action, to make room in his life and art for a decisive change. In November 1936, he gave away the little Cézanne *Three Bathers*, his companion for so many years, to the Petit Palais Museum. Only a year or two before, Albert Barnes had offered Matisse more than $60,000 for this painting, but Matisse had refused to part with it. The Cézanne was not only dear to him as a painting, it had become his lodestar, his talisman—reminders of it ran through some of his greatest achievements. The seated figures in the Barnes mural, for instance, are related to the seated figure on the right in *Three Bathers*. And the four huge bronze bas-reliefs of the female back, done by Matisse between 1909 and 1930, work steadily toward the same sort of simplification that Cézanne achieved in the backs of his painted bathers.

Much as he loved the Cézanne, Matisse may have felt in 1936 that he no longer needed it. Perhaps, in giving it to the museum, he thought it might serve others as it had served him. In a letter to the museum's director, he claimed to know the picture "fairly well, I hope, but not completely." He also said that he considered it "a very solid, very complete realization of a composition that [Cézanne] carefully studied in other canvases." But Matisse had done all he wanted to do with solidity and sculptural form. Ever since the composition of the Barnes mural, when he had used cut-paper shapes to plan his design, something had changed in his creative method and in his ambitions.

The new direction of his work can best be seen in *Pink Nude*, a painting begun in May 1935 and completed some six months later, and in the series of 22 photographs taken of it while it was in progress *(pages 134-135)*. In the charcoal sketches for *Pink Nude*, the model is drawn realistically and is a creature of great power and physical splendor. Matisse's main problem, in translating this magnificent animal of a woman into paint, was apparently in adjusting her to her background. What sort of a background should she have? And how should she be modified so that her figure and her background were integrated? Matisse rehearsed this problem, with various cut-paper solutions, much as a theater director rehearses a particularly tricky scene by playing it in a variety of ways. In the first version the model is simply a naked woman lying on a couch in what is recognizably a room; there is space between the couch and the wall, and if the model rolled off the far side of the couch she would be hidden from view.

Little by little, in subsequent versions, Matisse compressed the space between the couch and the wall, and finally tilted the couch upward, so that both couch and wall are in the same plane. The model changed too, until in the end she was anatomically all wrong. No head ever sat on a body like this, as if it were a turret, and no shoulder and elbow and forearm ever joined together to form what looks like a triumphal arch. Matisse has everywhere adjusted and simplified. Where the model originally lolled in the middle distance, well back from the picture plane, in the final painting she is so far forward that she seems about to fall off the canvas into the viewer's lap. For that matter, her pose is no longer suggestive of indolence. The left leg is drawn up as if she means to spring from the couch, and the set of her head and left elbow are emblems of vigilance.

By 1938 Matisse was beginning to use cut paper not merely as a working device, but as an end in itself. Instead of serving as a preparatory step to painting, it had become painting's replacement. In the little picture called *The Dancer*, which he made and gave to Leonide Massine in May 1938, Matisse put aside the brushes and oil paints that he had labored so long to master, and used scissors alone. It was not a complete abdication—he was still to do many beautiful easel paintings—but it was an alternative. But before that alternative could be fully explored, Western Europe was overwhelmed by an event that everyone had dreaded, but in some ways had almost longed for: war with Hitler's Germany. In the face of war, even the most determinedly private lives are interrupted. To this, Matisse was no exception.

The first magazine covers Matisse designed were for the front and back of the luxurious French periodical *Minotaure*, a review devoted mostly to Surrealist writing and art. The front cover *(top)* reflects Surrealism's interest in expressing subconscious feelings by fantasy or unexpected juxtaposition; for it, Matisse scattered the letters of the magazine title across features that might belong to man or beast. For the back cover *(above)*, he drew with a few flawless lines the Minotaur, the legendary half-man, half-bull that was adopted as the Surrealists' symbol.

Matisse the Designer

Matisse periodically refreshed his creative energies by turning from painting or sculpture to other forms of expression. And each time he did so, the change in media became more than diversion, for it led to great art of a new and striking kind. In the 1930s, Matisse used his skill at drawing and his inherent sense of design to illustrate books, thus linking himself with the other modern French painters from Édouard Manet to Raoul Dufy, who had put their art at the service of literature. Then, in the 1940s, Matisse summoned all his talents in producing the designs —stained-glass windows, ceramic tile murals, sculpture, even the vestments—for a small Dominican chapel at Vence in the south of France.

Matisse's first full-fledged efforts at book illustration were for an edition of the works of the late 19th Century poet Stéphane Mallarmé. Commissioned by the Swiss publisher Albert Skira, the book was to be the second in a series done by important contemporary artists, the first of whom was Matisse's friendly rival, Picasso. Using etchings in this first work, Matisse later made lithographs and, for the picture at right, he used the linoleum-cut technique. Never content merely to provide illustrations for his books, Matisse invariably took a hand in designing the jackets, selecting the typeface—he hand-lettered one text —and choosing the paper and binding. In much the same way he became totally involved when he designed the interior of the Vence Chapel, a project that occupied him for almost four years during his last decade.

With a few white lines on a black ground, Matisse expressed the sensual beauty of Pasiphaë, legendary queen of King Minos of ancient Crete and the heroine of a tragic play, written by the modern French novelist Henry de Montherlant. Her hair falls from her horned crown in labyrinthine curls that suggest chains binding her to her monstrous fate as mother of the Minotaur.

Linoleum-cut frontispiece for *Pasiphaé —Chant de Minos* (from *Les Crétois* by Henry de Montherlant), 1937-1944

A Bibliophile's Books

Matisse claimed that he had been a bibliophile before he even owned a book, and he approached the designing of books with a special sensitivity to the writer's intent.

In the works shown on these pages, Matisse celebrated the springtime of French poetry—the 15th and 16th Centuries. He did so at a time when he was old and ill and Europe was locked in World War II. The war almost put an end to the work below, Matisse's design for a book of verse of Pierre de Ronsard, the 16th Century lyricist. The occupation of France isolated Matisse from his Swiss publisher, and not until the War was over could they continue their work on the book. Then it was discovered that the printed pages were yellowed; simple reprinting was impossible because the type used was worn, and the book was delayed once again. It was finally published in 1948, seven years after Matisse had started work on it.

In the elegy below, the poet Ronsard begged an artist to portray his beloved without flattery, asserting that only an ugly woman needs the artifice of paint and painters. Matisse responded with a demure and lovely portrait. For the verses of Charles, Duke of Orléans, a valiant military leader in the 15th Century and the last master of French courtly poetry *(right)*, Matisse created a hand-lettered title page to face his lithograph of Charles' noble, arrogant profile and decorated the poems with a rococo border, heraldic insignia and the fleur-de-lis emblem of France's royal line.

On the following pages are two of Matisse's illustrations for his first commissioned book design. Tiny symbolic figures and clean-lined etched portraits of Charles Baudelaire and Edgar Allan Poe, the poet's literary idols, faced pages of Mallarmé's opaque elusive verse.

ÉLÉGIE A JANET
Peintre du Roy

PEIN moy, Janet, pein moy je te supplie,
Sur ce tableau les beautez de m'amie
De la façon que je te les diray.
Comme importun je ne te suppliray
D'un art menteur quelque faveur luy faire.
Il suffit bien si tu la sçais portraire
Ainsi qu'elle est, sans vouloir desguiser
Son naturel pour la favoriser :
Car la faveur n'est bonne que pour celles
Qui se font peindre, et qui ne sont pas belles.

30

"Élégie à Janet" and lithograph from *Florilège des Amours de Ronsard,* 1941-1948

Frontispiece and title page from *Poèmes de Charles d'Orléans*, 1943-1950

Lithograph from *Poèmes de Charles d'Orléans*, 1943-1950

"Le tombeau de Charles Baudelaire" from *Poésies de Stéphane Mallarmé*, 1932

"Le tombeau d'Edgar Poe" from *Poésies de Stéphane Mallarmé*, 1932

Matisse rearranges the scale model of the chapel.

A chapel by Matisse

In 1947 a Dominican nun, who some years earlier had nursed Matisse after an operation, shyly asked his advice about her design for a stained-glass window. The window was to be in a chapel that her order was going to build in Vence, a small hill town where Matisse lived for most of his later years. The master began suggesting changes, but soon he became fired by the challenge of the entire project—the architectural plan, the construction materials, the furniture, even the priest's robes. Offering to work without pay and to submit to church authorities for approval, Matisse plunged ahead.

Designing and redesigning from scale models (*above*) and using cut paper as his sketches for windows—a technique he had pioneered in the murals for the Barnes Foundation (*pages 130-131*)—Matisse perfected a plan of balanced volumes and forms. (For Matisse, the challenge was that of creating a graphic poem, expressing a complex idea in a rigid form as his beloved poets had done in verse.) He seemed to thrive on the strict requirements of designing a chapel and he rose to the physical demands of such large-scale work.

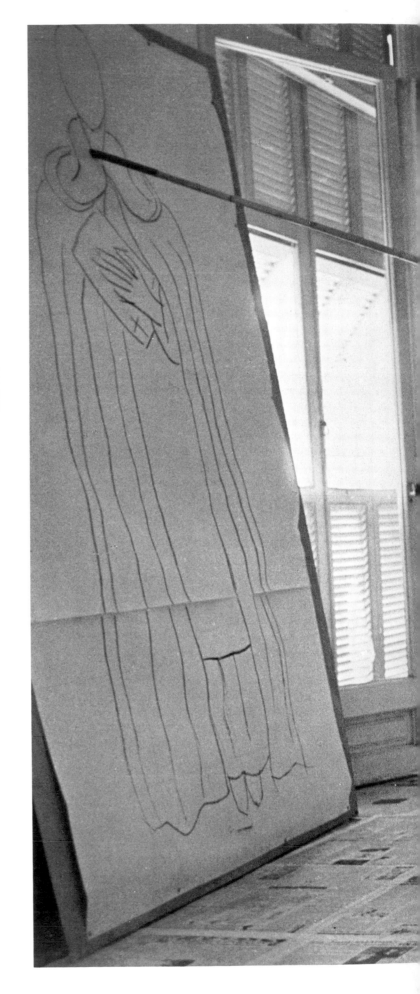

Using a bamboo pole tipped with charcoal, Matisse draws a half-scale figure of St. Dominic. Behind him are his drawings for the Stations of the Cross.

Matisse's square-set white stucco chapel *(left)* fits its hot, sunny site as easily as any age-old Mediterranean building. From the bright carpet of low-growing plants around it to the Madonna and Child inset over the twin sanctuary windows and the wrought-iron spire, Matisse designed, sculpted, drew and meticulously oversaw its every outer detail, even to the landscaping. But it is inside that he fulfilled his aim: balancing, as he said, "a surface of light and color against a solid white wall covered with black drawings," so that each contrasting element

enhances the other. Matisse drew the sweeping, ink-black lines of the murals on ceramic tiles that were then glazed and mounted on three walls in the church. Their shining surfaces seem to come alive in the varicolored light flooding through the stained-glass windows.

As the worshiper enters the chapel *(below)* he faces the blue, green and gold windows that glow behind the altar and the serene figure of St. Dominic, the order's founder, that towers beside it. To the viewer's right, on a long tiled wall, the Virgin Mary, surrounded by a flock of cloudlike flowers, holds the Christ child, His arms outspread in a gesture that foreshadows the Crucifixion. As the worshiper turns again, back toward the door through which he entered, he faces the 14 Stations of the Cross *(below, right)*. There, instead of picturing those scenes in the customary procession, Matisse chose to condense the story of Christ's Passion in a single dramatic composition. Its terse symbolism includes, in the miraculous imprint of Christ's face on St. Veronica's kerchief *(number 6)*, the only detailed features represented in the bold murals.

On the altar of the Vence chapel, the worshiper sees a slender bronze Crucifix (*above*), flanked by six tall candlesticks. Matisse's Christ is dead, but the sculpture is so stylized and ethereal that only the limp arms and drooping head suggest His agony.

On the viewer's left as he faces the altar (*photograph at right*), the wooden choir stalls that Matisse designed for the nuns are set into a secluded alcove for their devotions. The artist arranged the simple stone altar at an angle so that the officiating priest faces both the nuns and the lay congregation, who stand and kneel—there are no pews—in the marble-floored body of the church. Behind the nuns' enclave, nine narrow stained-glass windows echo the pointed leaves of the Tree of Life motif in the windows that dominate the chapel wall at the worshiper's left.

Matisse's accomplishment in the Vence chapel is the more remarkable since he himself had never been close to the Church. Yet he imbued his creation with an austere joy. Matisse once observed that if an afterlife existed, he would like to think of it as "a Paradise where I would paint frescoes."

161

VIII

The Prophecy Fulfilled

Watched by one of his models, the aged Matisse works with a pair of long-bladed scissors on his colored paper cutouts. He was confined to bed and wheelchair by a severe intestinal illness, but continued to experiment with cut-paper designs of natural forms in bold colors. In the last few years of his life he elevated this seemingly simple recreation to a form that caught the fancy of the entire art world.

When World War II broke out in September 1939, Matisse was four months short of his 70th birthday. Too old to take an active part in the war, he was nevertheless deeply distressed by this third German attempt within his own lifetime to overrun his country. The invasion of France in 1940 came as an appalling blow to him. He was living in Paris at the time, and as the German armies drew nearer the city, he allayed his disquiet by taking himself off to the movies every night, becoming a compulsive moviegoer. As for the calamitous years after the fall of France, he bore them as stoically as possible.

In this he differed from several of his former colleagues. Vlaminck, for example, felt authorized by the French collapse to indulge in outbursts of anti-Semitism. Derain—now a thoroughgoing traditionalist— was deceived into exhibiting his work in Germany and into making an official visit to Berlin, on the understanding that by so doing he could secure the release of French prisoners of war. For this collaboration he was ostracized by most of his former friends after the war and ended his days in obscurity. In 1954 he blundered into the path of a passing car on the road outside his house near Paris, and died of his injuries.

Matisse could not be gulled into cooperating with the Germans during the occupation, but neither could he be stampeded into demanding revenge against the collaborators after France was liberated. "I cannot see," he wrote in the fall of 1944, when he heard that Vlaminck had been arrested, "why we should torture people because they don't think as we do." More than once he was urged to go abroad—his son Pierre in New York was one of many people who would have welcomed him. But he turned down every offer. In 1940, with a visa in his pocket for Brazil, he wrote Pierre: "When I saw everything in such a mess I had them reimburse my ticket. I realized that I should have felt like a deserter. If everyone who is worth anything leaves France, what will remain of our country?"

When the Germans entered Paris in June 1940, Matisse headed back for Nice by a circuitous route. July found him in the little town of Saint-Gaudens, near the Pyrennees. He had been in poor health for some time, and in Saint-Gaudens he had an attack of enteritis that filled him with foreboding. "I could have died like a rat in a trap," he said later, for "the good, sympathetic old doctor . . . didn't see what was wrong." By August he was back in Nice, but he simply had no strength to go on painting. "I await the thunderbolt which cannot fail to come," he wrote his son. In January 1941 he was taken to the Clinique du Parc in Lyons, where he was operated on twice by one of the greatest surgeons in Europe, René Leriche. Matisse came through this operation, but only just. The Dominican sisters who nursed him spoke of him as "the man who came back from the dead." The disease had been allowed to spread too far, and one wall of his abdomen was damaged so severely that he would never again be able to stand upright for more than a few minutes at a time. One thing sustained him through the cruel three months in the hospital: the thought of his apartment in Nice, and the hope that he might one day be permitted to go back to it.

In 1938 Matisse had given up his quarters in the old town of Nice for a suite of rooms in the Hotel Regina, high above the city in the suburb of Cimiez. The Regina had been built at the turn of the century in expectation of regular visits from Queen Victoria. It had the ample comforts and majestic proportions typical of grand hotels of that era, and Matisse, in his spacious rooms, had recreated his own small world. He often spoke of it to his nurses in the Lyons hospital, describing to them his prized possessions, things he had accumulated and kept with him over a period of more than 50 years.

Among the possessions were paintings by Courbet, Cézanne and Picasso, an ancient Greek statue of Apollo from Delphi and the fragment of very old Oriental carpet that he had framed under glass and hung on the wall. He also spoke of a favorite tobacco jar, labeled "Tabac Royal," of the pewter jug that appears in so many of his paintings, of his own early bronze sculpture, *The Serf*. He told them about his collection of Coromandel lacquerwork from India, his African masks and fetishes, his Korean pots and Han Dynasty dancing figures, and the Persian embroideries that reminded him of his enthusiasm for Islamic art, some 30 years before.

Matisse identified with the furnishings of the places in which he lived to a quite extraordinary degree. A chair could capture his imag-

The glass case at right contains many of the objects that Matisse immortalized in his painting. They were collected after his death for the Matisse Museum in Cimiez near Nice. Among the most familiar are the jar labeled "Tabac Royal" (royal tobacco) at lower left, the pewter jug at the right on the top row and the tall, patterned earthenware vase beside it. Matisse cherished his artistic chattels and kept them with him for many years, even as he moved from place to place. The vase with two large handles just under the tall crock appears in a painting that he executed as early as 1903.

ination for weeks on end. He never forgot the Victorian rocking chair in his hotel room in Tahiti, or the curved and scrolled red armchair that he had once seen in a house at a French resort on the Atlantic coast. In 1942 he wrote the poet and novelist Louis Aragon of his joy at acquiring a particular kind of chair, one that he had wanted for a year. "It is a Venetian Baroque chair, it's silver toned with varnish, like enamel. . . . When I met it in an antique shop, a few weeks ago, I was quite overcome by it. It is splendid. . . ."

In one room of the Regina apartment Matisse kept his aviaries, which sometimes harbored as many as 300 birds. On occasion he also owned a company of free-flying white doves, one of which, given as a gift to Picasso, served as the model for Picasso's famous 1949 lithograph. Matisse, who was in general canny about money (he was always advising his fellow artists to "Buy gold!"), was extravagant when it came to birds and never regretted it. Visitors to his apartment remember the Bengalis, the cardinals, the Japanese nightingales, the long black plumage of the widow birds, the blinding whiteness of the doves.

Beyond the aviaries was a winter garden—really a small-scale jungle with huge-leaved Tahitian philodendron and a profusion of exotic shrubs, plants and flowers. Matisse spent a great deal of time tending them. "By looking after them," he told one visitor, "I get to know the weight, the needs and the character of every one of them, and that helps me when I come to draw them." Students, he observed on another occasion, would do better to spend their time in zoos and botanical gardens than in art schools. Among live plants and animals "they can learn the secrets of embryonic life, and little by little acquire that mysterious *fluide* that every authentic artist acquires in the end."

· Matisse's old studio in the elegant, old-fashioned Hotel Regina in Cimiez looks out over the hotel's gardens toward the rich Mediterranean blue of Nice's Bay of Angels, a view he painted many times. Even the writhing Art Nouveau railings of his balcony, where he sunned the many plants he kept in his suite, are reminders of his love of complex pattern and sinuous line.

By August 1940 Matisse was back in this world he had created for himself in the Hotel Regina. Shuffling from room to room in his tea-planter's pajamas, he was more chary than ever of wasting his time. The outer world tempted him hardly at all. Sometimes he would go down to the secluded jungle garden built above the port of St. Jean-Cap Ferrat by his friend Tériade, the publisher of the art periodical *Verve*, or to the garden of the Hotel Regina, where, he said, "Everything is new, everything is fresh, as if the world had just been born. A flower, a leaf, a pebble, they all shine, they all glisten, lustrous, varnished. . . ." But in general it tired him to go visiting. His concentration on his work was so single-minded that he no longer even enjoyed going over to Roquebrune to see his old friend Simon Bussy when the Bussys had other guests. The guests were usually literary people, "quite a strange crowd to me"; he could not "chat and be intimate in a circle in which no one understands painting."

Before long he was working as hard as ever, from nine to twelve every morning, seven days of the week, and again in the afternoon from two until nightfall. Although this was one of the blackest moments in Europe's history, no one would have guessed it from his paintings. Picasso at the time was complaining of the ever-increasing shortage of food, and was painting fleshless carcasses. Braque was alluding to the rundown condition of his household, and was painting debristled

Among the most unusual forms in which Matisse expressed his art is the three-by-five-foot rug, "Mimosa," that he designed for the American firm of Alexander Smith Carpets. Matisse had long been fascinated by the way light is caught and reflected in pile carpets—he had framed and hung several old Persian rugs like paintings—and he attacked the commission enthusiastically. His central motif, based on the golden plumes of blossom that cover mimosa trees in the Riviera's early spring, is surrounded by blue, gray and black designs on a ground of rectangles in various shades of red. Only a limited number of these brilliant rugs were made. Not surprisingly, most of them are displayed as wall hangings rather than used on the floor.

brooms. But Matisse was painting paradise. In these paintings, done between 1941 and 1943, he seems not to have had a thought in his head beyond the balance of a Christmas rose against a saxifrage plant. Nothing is soiled or worn or in short supply. There are always enough oysters and oranges, the slipcovers are freshly laundered and the floors freshly waxed, and beautiful women can still count on owning a new dress.

The pictures looked so misleadingly easy that when Matisse assembled a group of them for a special issue of *Verve*, he included beside each picture a diagram analyzing its color—like a great general in retirement, giving away the secrets of his strategy. Matisse, however, had not so much retired as arrived—although "arrival" was a word that made him shiver. "Arrival = Prison," he wrote in his seventies, "and the artist must never be a prisoner. A prisoner of his own self, prisoner of a way of painting, prisoner of his reputation, prisoner of success, and so on. . . . Was it not the Goncourts who said that the Japanese painters of the great period changed their names several times during their lives? I like that; they wanted to safeguard their liberties."

Matisse never changed his name, but he did repeatedly change his way of painting and his reputation, and in 1943 there were intimations that he was about to do so again. "All the signs indicate that I am about to start working on large-scale compositions, as if I had the whole of life, or another life, before me," he told Louis Aragon. Here was Matisse, pushing 74 and unable even to stand at an easel, planning to work on the scale of Tintoretto. It didn't make sense. But Matisse believed in historical inevitability: if the idea of painting a large-scale composition had come to him, then a way would be found to act upon the idea. "We are not the masters of what we do," he once said, "what we do is imposed upon us." Destiny had imposed upon him the duty of once again working on a large scale, and somehow he would fulfill it.

Meanwhile, destiny intervened in his life in quite another way. In March 1943 Cimiez was bombed by the Allies. Though the raid was trifling as such things go, it was expected to be the first of many. Matisse was advised to decamp, and decamp he did—to a small villa called Le Rêve on the outskirts of the little town of Vence, up in the hills behind Nice. This was to be his home for six years.

Le Rêve was too small to accommodate a large-scale project, and in any case the war was encroaching upon his life in ways that were most upsetting. In the spring of 1944 he received word that Madame Matisse and his daughter Madame Duthuit had been taken prisoner separately, in different places. Both had been working for the French Resistance, and were arrested for knowing what they should not have known and passing it on where it could do most good. Marguerite Duthuit in particular had a very bad time of it. She was tortured by the Gestapo and put on a prison train headed for the concentration camp at Ravensbruck. Luckily an Allied air raid prevented the train from reaching its destination, and eventually Madame Duthuit found her way back to Paris. Madame Matisse was sentenced to six months in prison in Troyes. "I am hoping," wrote Matisse to his old friend Charles Camoin, "that the three months of arrest will count in her sentence."

At the same time he worried about his son Jean, living just outside Paris in Vanves. "He lives in the suburb so badly bombed, and he gives me no news . . ." wrote Matisse. Although Jean's silence did not exactly surprise him, "for I was like him when young . . . I loved my parents, but was very slack in writing," still he had not heard from his son in almost a month—the month of the Normandy invasion.

Then, in August 1944, Vence itself felt the effects of the war. When the Allies landed a second invasion force on the Mediterranean coast between Marseilles and Nice, three stray shells fell near Matisse's home in the middle of the night. He was not unduly distressed. "I went down into a comfortable shelter trench in the garden, in which I remained for 36 hours—quite undisturbed," he wrote. It gave him a chance to read the philosophy of Henri Bergson, "which I had only skimmed at home, distracted by the drawings and paintings on the walls around me." Matisse's keepsake from this experience was an olive twig, symbol of peace, which was blown through the window by the exploding shell and landed beside his bed.

At Vence, Matisse found a new project to occupy his mind. Ever since his hospital stay at Lyons he had wanted somehow to express his gratitude to the Dominican nuns who had nursed him back to health with such exemplary care and skill. Initially he had thought of building a chapel for the Order at its headquarters at Gramond. But just across the road from his villa at Vence there was a Dominican rest home for invalid girls, and the chapel of this home had recently been destroyed in a fire. By a curious coincidence one of the nuns attached to the home was one of his former nurses from Lyons, Sister Jacques. In a modest way she too was an artist, and one day on a visit to Le Rêve she brought with her a sketch for a stained-glass window for the new chapel. Matisse became interested, and before long it was agreed that he should design the new building. A Dominican monk with some architectural training, Brother Rayssiguier, acted as his consultant on both structural and liturgical matters, and Auguste Perret, dean of modern French architects, also provided some advice. Fundamentally, however, the Chapelle du Rosaire belongs to Matisse.

The chance to put art into the mainstream of life has tempted many modern painters to accept large-scale commissions for public buildings, but few have done so successfully. Picasso will not be remembered for his murals for the UNESCO building in Paris, nor will Bonnard and Vuillard for their decorations in the League of Nations building in Geneva. In their eagerness, they tried too hard, and the results often turned out to be inflated versions of their easel paintings, not suited to the task at hand. Matisse made no such mistake. The Vence chapel is quite unlike any of his other work. With his unequaled mastery of opulent color and complicated design, he could easily have taken a space as large as Grand Central Station and made it vibrate like a steel mill in wartime. Instead he made the Vence chapel so modest that some visitors are dismayed. Many of its surfaces are unadorned white, and the light that filters into the chapel through tall, narrow windows is for most of the day pale and diffused.

The Abby Aldrich Rockefeller Memorial Window in the Union Church of Pocantico Hills, New York, is Matisse's last completed work. Working in Nice with paper cutouts as his model for the stained-glass window, the aged artist combined white and soft yellows, blues and greens to suggest the idea of light as the prime creator. Matisse was absorbed, he wrote, "by the challenge to express myself in a defined and limited space, and to harmonize my composition not only with the form of the actual framework but also with the atmosphere of the chapel"—a building he knew only from the photographs and architectural drawings that were sent to him.

Not content merely to create windows and wall decorations for the Chapel of the Rosary at Vence, Matisse also designed some 20 bright chasubles—the simple hooded outer garments worn by priests when celebrating mass. He worked with paper cutouts (shown on his studio wall above and below), basing their motifs on traditional religious images—crosses, stars, palm fronds and natural forms. When Picasso saw them he was so struck by the brilliant colors that he suggested Matisse design capes for bullfighters.

Typically, Matisse made a great many preliminary sketches for the chapel, and the progress of these sketches is invariably from complex to simple, from turbulent to tranquil, from particular to general, from many to few. The design for the windows began as an ecstatic Heavenly Jerusalem and ended as a serene Tree of Life; the Stations of the Cross was originally a richly detailed costume drama, but the final design is a black-and-white drawing that looks like the urgent notes of an eyewitness to Christ's passion. The floor, which Matisse at first meant to ornament with rosettes outlined in red, in the end is composed of slabs of white marble with small squares of black set into the corners. Even the number of windows was reduced by four from the original count of 19. Matisse was everywhere out to dematerialize.

At first sight the chapel seems a place full of color, but in fact the only color comes from the stained-glass windows. Matisse, a master at coloring flat surfaces, has here filled an interior space with wraiths of color, phantoms of yellow and green and blue, constantly in motion. Even the glass itself has an incorporeal quality. The chapel is just this side of having no physical existence at all; it is not the expression of a great artist at play, but of a great man, halfway to paradise.

Nearly 50 years before, Matisse had spoken in "A Painter's Notes" of an art of "balance, purity and serenity." The chapel exemplifies those qualities precisely. But it also exemplifies an unfeigned humility. Matisse did not want to make the building simply a work of art, he also wanted to make it a working chapel. Some people concluded from this that he had abandoned the attitudes of a lifetime to return to the Church. Not everyone was pleased. "Very pretty, very gay," said his friend Louis Aragon, a Communist, after examining the model. "When we come into power, we'll turn it into a dance hall." But the eminent Catholic writer Henri Daniel-Rops felt sure the chapel was an act of faith. "The Christian," he wrote, "finds here nothing between himself and God." Matisse himself settled the matter. "The only religion I have is my love of the work that I have to do, my love of creation, and my love of absolute sincerity. I made the chapel to express myself completely, and for no other reason."

One of the things that most delighted Matisse about the chapel was the color—the way it moved around, changed with the weather, lived its own life. (It was at its sharpest and finest, he thought, at 11 o'clock on a winter's morning.) Nothing quite comparable could be done with paints and canvas, but surely there might be some middle way—a way to let color fly free, as a pigeon flies from the hand? There was indeed such a way, and it had been right under Matisse's nose for some time. In 1941 he had pinned colored papers to a canvas to create a still life of fruit and household objects on a table. Then he had drawn on the papers, painted them, and stretched two lengths of string across the top and bottom of the canvas to indicate the table. In no time at all and with nothing, or almost nothing, he had created an image that normally he would have toiled over for a month or more. His scissors had done the drawing, the color remained free and the composition was as firm as if it had been elaborately worked out with paint.

Matisse did not turn exclusively to this new kind of picture-making until he went back to the Hotel Regina in Cimiez at the end of the war. But he did use it in the meantime for the most fateful of all his illustrated books: *Jazz*. Unlike the other books for which he had provided only pictures, *Jazz* contained text supplied by Matisse himself. The words' meaning was secondary, for their principal function was purely visual. They were, he said, a restful accompaniment to the colors in the pictures, serving the same purpose as "a small bunch of asters in a bouquet of grander flowers." For the pictures he drew upon his "memories of the circus, memories of folk-tales, memories of travel" to create brilliantly colored fantasies. "The Cowboy," for instance *(page 174)*, is a fantasy of violent action in which man and horse are joined together by an imperious lariat. "Icarus" is a fantasy of disaster in which the doomed aeronaut falls through a night sky starred with yellow. "Lagoon" is Matisse's first reference, after 20 years, to the underwater life he had observed in Tahiti.

The title for the book, *Jazz*, was chosen because it suited the pictures' discordant cross-rhythms, but it also happened to suit Matisse's chosen mode of expression. He wanted to jot down his ideas spontaneously, in the same quicksilver, elliptical way they came to him, and he wanted to improvise cross-references—relating one shape to another on the spur of the moment. Scissors and paper provided the answer. The designs he sent to the printer were made by cutting into large sheets of paper colored in advance with watercolors so brilliant that his doctor recommended he wear dark glasses when he entered his studio. None of the shapes was drawn in the conventional sense; all the work was done with scissors.

For Matisse, *Jazz* was a liberation. When he cut into the pure color he felt, he said, like a sculptor cutting into marble. The pictures had a crisp liveliness, a delight in short cuts and epigrams for the eye; he was free to be satirical and unpredictably inventive. *Jazz* also freed him to face the day when he could no longer work at the easel. When that dreaded day came, there would still be a way he could make pictures—perhaps even the big pictures he had mentioned to Louis Aragon.

On December 31, 1949, Matisse was 80, a suitable occasion for tributes, and many were forthcoming. But often they carried a backward-looking, valedictory note. Matisse was known best for his Nice paintings—pictures of languorous odalisques in high-ceilinged Mediterranean rooms—and these were now associated with what people considered a frivolous era in French life. Matisse was regarded, quite unjustly, as the Boucher or Fragonard of a ruling class that had put self before country and had gone down forever in 1939. Besides, he was said to be very ill, and it was known that he could no longer sit at his easel. It seemed most unlikely that Matisse could be expected to produce anything more of much consequence.

Visitors to the Hotel Regina did indeed find the artist propped up in bed, unable even to perambulate the miniature forest in which he had once taken such pride. But Matisse was not inactive. The walls of his bedroom were covered from floor to ceiling with forms cut out of colored paper. Sometimes they were fixed to canvas, sometimes they were tacked on the wall, sometimes they dangled down and trailed onto the floor. "Now that I don't often get up," he said, "I've made myself a little garden to go for walks in. Everything's there—fruit and flowers and leaves, a bird or two. . . . " Above his head, on the ceiling, he had drawn some larger-than-life-size women's heads in charcoal: "They keep me company too," he said. "It was no trouble . . . I had someone tie the charcoal to the end of that fishing rod over there, and then I went to work."

Matisse had known about these alternatives to easel painting for years —ever since he had prepared the mural for the Barnes Foundation. Now, suddenly, in his 80s, he realized that they could help him turn a handicap—his physical condition—into an advantage. Bedridden, cut off from the paints and brushes that had been mastered only after a lifetime of work, he could have foundered in self-pity or settled for a hard-earned idleness. Instead he went on working as hard as ever, and in the last five years of his life re-invented for himself a way of painting that younger artists all over the world were to adopt after his death.

The mechanics of this method were fairly simple: Matisse had sheets of paper painted under his direction, and then cut into them with shears in a way that was half-drawing, half-sculpting. When he had the exact forms he wanted, he told an assistant where to put them; when all the pieces of paper were placed to his liking, he had them fastened onto canvas. The result was art of a peculiarly exhilarating sort. Sometimes the cut-paper compositions were related to his earlier work, sometimes not. In them, for instance, he finally perfected the effortless flowing movement of the human body in action, a movement he had been striving for ever since the *Dance* mural for Shchukin, back in 1909. No painting of bodies in motion was ever as convincing as the cut-paper bodies in *The Swimming Pool*, a huge, panoramic composition more than 50 feet long. These bodies have the relaxed power of great jungle cats: looking at their contours it is clear what Matisse meant when he referred to his cut papers as carvings.

It is an extraordinary experience to stand in front of one of these big cut-paper pictures. There is, first of all, the sheer size of the imagery. In all but a few of his previous works, Matisse had concentrated upon nuances of line and color; here he is concentrating upon physical scale. Nothing he had done before is anything like these elongated black women, this sea siren stranded in the topmost branches of a tropical forest, this sailboat scudding beneath lavender-edged clouds, these swimmers kicking their way—like so many porpoises—half-in, half-out of a band of pellucid water. Matisse's shears cut into his imagination as well as into the paper. These enormous pictures are like enormous sighs of exhilaration as Matisse at last sighted the Promised Land: the complete simplification of painting.

In the cut papers Matisse finally realized the ideal of pure color that had been glimpsed by the Impressionists, analyzed by the Pointillists, fought for by the Fauves, and exploited by the German Expressionists. Here was color on its own—pure untrammeled, uncompromising—commanding attention in itself and for itself. Matisse gave up a great deal to get it. Like Tamino, the hero of Mozart's opera *The Magic Flute*, he put himself through a symbolic ordeal, abandoned almost all the things that had carried him through life: he renounced the orthodox ways of managing paint and canvas, the minute and loving preparation of composition, the subtleties of tone, the indications of space and scale. In doing so he discovered that "the energy within you is stronger than ever for being held back, compressed, and said No to." But to make it work successfully, he added, "you also have to have a long previous experience, and that experience must not have blunted your instincts."

In his late 80s Matisse was still the same man who had painted *Joy of Life* and *Dance* and *Music*, the *Pink Nude* and *Large Red Interior*. But he saw no point in repeating them. He was like a traveler who had crossed the frontier into a new country, leaving his baggage behind—or like the Japanese painters who changed their names so as not to be weighed down by what they had done in the past. The cut-paper compositions were the work of a man very near death, but they were like signals from the springtime of life. All over the world they were taken up as symbols of absolute purity and clarity. Every painter today who uses color simply and directly is in some way indebted to Matisse; at 80, he was the painter other painters needed. But if this last dazzling work is now regarded as the work most worth looking at, this is a misconception that time will one day set right. For Matisse was always a painter to watch, and the world has still to take the full measure of what it lost when on November 3, 1954, the heart of Henri Matisse came to a stop.

Sketching one of his favorite doves, the 82-year-old Matisse relaxes in his Nice apartment in 1951. This superb photograph of the bespectacled old master was made by the great French photojournalist Henri Cartier-Bresson. Photographer and painter became good friends, and one of Matisse's last efforts in book illustration was the design of the covers for Cartier-Bresson's collection of photographs called *The Decisive Moment*.

Carving with Color

An old man cutting up brightly colored paper might seem to be frittering away his final years with the pastimes of a child. Yet colored paper and scissors in the hands of one old man—Henri Matisse—produced great art. Matisse's colored paper cutouts seem to generate their own sunlight; their wry simplicity is so typical of the artist that they provide a fitting conclusion to his lifework.

Matisse came upon colored cutouts almost by accident. In the 1930s he had used paper models to help design his paintings, moving them around on his canvases to find the perfect placement of figures. Then in 1941, when he was 72 years old, a serious intestinal illness and two complicated operations left him an invalid for the rest of his life. Propped up in his bed, he began to make cutouts because he could no longer paint at an easel. But they became more than a simple substitute for painting. "To cut right into color makes me think of a sculptor's carving into stone," he wrote of his new art. Using his scissors as he might a chisel, Matisse carved human figures, leaves, flowers and fish, and imaginative arabesques. He then placed the cutouts on white or multicolored backgrounds, manipulating them until they harmonized. Some stood as completed pictures; others were models for decorative tiles, stained-glass windows, posters and magazine covers. All are charged with Matisse's clarity of vision; they remain the final monuments to a master of design and color.

Matisse's quest for simplicity found expression in this paper cutout of a female nude, done in 1950 when the artist was 81. It is a huge picture—almost eight feet high—its character reflecting Matisse's admiration of prehistoric and primitive art, whose bold, abstract qualities had long fascinated him.

Zulma, 1950

Matisse had experimented with cutouts for several years, but it was not until 1947, when he published a book called *Jazz*, that he proved he had mastered this new art form. *Jazz*, which took about three years to complete, is a collection of abstracted colored cutouts like those shown here. It includes a text written by Matisse and printed in his own commanding longhand script. The text, unrelated to the cutouts, consists of gentle truths and observations about art and life; chatty but incisive, it is intended mainly to provide the viewer's eyes with a rest from the dazzling art. About the book itself, Matisse wrote, "The images, in vivid and violent tones, have resulted from crystallizations in memories of the circus, popular tales, or travel." These were his inspirations, but as he worked he became aware of an affinity between the lyrical quality of his pictures and the soaring improvisations of jazz music—thus the title of his book.

The cutouts themselves appear deceptively simple, but the technique of creating them was excruciatingly exact. Matisse explained, "Sometimes the difficulties appeared: lines, volumes, colors were put together, and then the whole thing collapsed, one part destroying another. . . . It is not enough to put colors against one another, however beautiful; the colors also have to react to one another. Otherwise, cacophony results. . . ." And it is the color that distinguishes all his cutouts. Matisse, dissatisfied with the limitations of commercial colored paper, created his own painted papers with hues so brilliant that his doctor warned the ailing artist not to enter his workroom without wearing dark glasses.

"The Cowboy," from *Jazz*

"The Toboggan," from *Jazz*

VERVE, NO. 35/36, THE LAST WORKS OF MATISSE

Christmas Night, 1952

Ivy in Flower, 1953

The paper cutout is the simplest and most direct way [I have found] of expressing myself up to now," Matisse said of his innovation. Delighting in this discovery, he filled his later years with a whirlwind of new projects. His ambitions, plans and energies seem appropriate to a young artist on the rise, rather than an established master in his eighties. Using his paper-cutout technique he designed tapestries, massive ceramic tiles and fanciful wall decorations; he was particularly fond of making models for stained-glass windows. The two shown here were commissioned by Time Inc. *(left)* and Mr. and Mrs. Albert D. Lasker *(above)*.

So popular did the Matisse cutouts become that in 1949 the Paris Museum of Modern Art devoted an entire exhibition to them, arousing an enthusiastic interest that soon led to other shows around the world. In 1953, just a year before he died, he completed *The Parakeet and the Siren (following pages)*, a gigantic composition about 12 by 25 feet that takes cutouts to dizzying heights of joy, lyricism and color orchestration.

177

Matisse's bedroom in his apartment in Nice

Matisse remained active until the day he died, although during his last two years he was confined mostly to his bed *(above)*. There, in his Riviera quarters, a scarf around his neck, wearing a faded gray sweater and peering through gold-rimmed glasses, he worked. When he was allowed to leave his bed, it was often to sit in a special chair placed before one of his last cutouts, a mammoth design for either a stained-glass window or a ceramic mural *(left)*. He was too weak to rise, and after he cut his figures or arabesques from the colored paper, he would tell his secretary, Lydia Delektorskaya, where to place each one. To alter his routine, he might model in clay *(right)*, returning to the medium he understood so well. Or he would draw while in bed, his charcoal pencil fixed to the end of a long bamboo pole. In this way, he completed many large sketches on paper pinned to the walls, as well as simple line drawings made directly on his walls and ceiling. Surrounded as he was by the faces he had drawn, Matisse said in his last days, "I am never alone."

The aged Matisse works on a clay model.

Chronology: Artists of Matisse's Era

1825 1900 1975 1825 1900 1975

FRANCE
PIERRE PUVIS DE CHAVANNES 1824-1898
WILLIAM-ADOLPHE BOUGUEREAU 1825-1905
GUSTAVE MOREAU 1826-1898
CAMILLE PISSARRO 1830-1903
ÉDOUARD MANET 1832-1883
EDGAR DEGAS 1834-1917
PAUL CÉZANNE 1839-1906
ODILON REDON 1840-1916
AUGUSTE RODIN 1840-1917
CLAUDE MONET 1840-1926
PIERRE-AUGUSTE RENOIR 1841-1919
PAUL GAUGUIN 1848-1903
GEORGES SEURAT 1859-1891
ARISTIDE MAILLOL 1861-1944
PAUL SIGNAC 1863-1935
HENRI DE TOULOUSE-LAUTREC 1864-1901
PIERRE BONNARD 1867-1947
ÉDOUARD VUILLARD 1868-1940
LOUIS VALTAT 1869-1952
HENRI MATISSE 1869-1954
MAURICE DENIS 1870-1943
GEORGES ROUAULT 1871-1958
ALBERT MARQUET 1876-1947
CONSTANTIN BRANCUSI 1876-1957
MAURICE DE VLAMINCK 1876-1958
RAOUL DUFY 1877-1953
FRANCIS PICABIA 1879-1953
ANDRÉ DERAIN 1880-1954
FERNAND LÉGER 1881-1955
GEORGES BRAQUE 1882-1963
MAURICE UTRILLO 1883-1955
ROBERT DELAUNAY 1885-1941
ANDRÉ LHOTE 1885-
JEAN ARP 1887-1966
MARCEL DUCHAMP 1887-1968
ANDRÉ MASSON 1896-
JEAN DUBUFFET 1901-
BALTHUS (BALTHASAR KLOSSOWSKI) 1908-
NICHOLAS DE STAËL 1914-1955

ITALY
CARLO CARRA 1881-1966
UMBERTO BOCCIONI 1882-1916
GINO SEVERINI 1883-1966
AMEDEO MODIGLIANI 1884-1920
GIORGIO DE CHIRICO 1888-
GIORGIO MORANDI 1890-1964

GERMANY
MAX LIEBERMANN 1847-1935
LOVIS CORINTH 1858-1925
EMIL NOLDE 1867-1956
LYONEL FEININGER 1871-1956
FRANZ MARC 1880-1916
ERNST LUDWIG KIRCHNER 1880-1938
MAX PECHSTEIN 1881-1955
ERICH HECKEL 1883-
MAX BECKMANN 1884-1950
KARL SCHMIDT-ROTTLUFF 1884-
AUGUST MACKE 1887-1914
KARL SCHWITTERS 1887-1948
LÁSZLÓ MOHOLY-NAGY 1895-1946

AUSTRIA
GUSTAV KLIMT 1862-1918
OSKAR KOKOSCHKA 1886-
EGON SCHIELE 1890-1918

HOLLAND
VINCENT VAN GOGH 1853-1890
PIET MONDRIAN 1872-1944

SWITZERLAND
PAUL KLEE 1879-1940

SPAIN
PABLO PICASSO 1881-
JUAN GRIS 1887-1927
JOAN MIRO 1893-
SALVADOR DALI 1904-

ENGLAND
WALTER RICHARD SICKERT 1860-1942
MATTHEW SMITH 1879-1959
BEN NICHOLSON 1894-
HENRY MOORE 1898-
FRANCIS BACON 1909-

SCANDINAVIA
EDVARD MUNCH 1863-1944

EASTERN EUROPE AND RUSSIA
ALEXEI VON JAWLENSKY 1864-1941
WASSILY KANDINSKY 1866-1944
FRANK KUPKA 1871-1957
CASIMIR MALEVICH 1878-1935
MARC CHAGALL 1889-
CHAIM SOUTINE 1894-1943

UNITED STATES
WINSLOW HOMER 1836-1910
THOMAS EAKINS 1844-1916
MARY CASSATT 1845-1926
ALBERT RYDER 1847-1917
JOHN SINGER SARGENT 1856-1925
CHILDE HASSAM 1859-1935
MAURICE PRENDERGAST 1861-1924
ROBERT HENRI 1865-1929
JOHN MARIN 1870-1953
JOHN SLOAN 1871-1951
MARSDEN HARTLEY 1877-1943
HANS HOFMANN 1880-1966
MAX WEBER 1881-1961
GEORGE BELLOWS 1882-1925
EDWARD HOPPER 1882-1967
CHARLES DEMUTH 1883-1935
CHARLES SHEELER 1883-1965
MARK TOBEY 1890-
MILTON AVERY 1893-
STUART DAVIS 1894-1964
ALEXANDER CALDER 1898-
MARK ROTHKO 1903-
ARSHILE GORKY 1904-1948
WILLEM DE KOONING 1904-
CLYFFORD STILL 1904-
DAVID SMITH 1906-1965
FRANZ KLINE 1910-1962
JACKSON POLLOCK 1912-1956
ROBERT MOTHERWELL 1915-
ROBERT RAUSCHENBERG 1925-
JASPER JOHNS 1930-

1825 1900 1975 1825 1900 1975

Matisse's predecessors, contemporaries and successors are grouped chronologically by country. The bands correspond to the artists' lifespans.

Bibliography

*Available in Paperback

MATISSE—HIS LIFE AND WORK

Barnes, Albert C., and Violette de Mazia, *The Art of Henri Matisse*. The Barnes Foundation Press. 1933.

Barr, Alfred M., *Matisse: His Art and His Public*. The Museum of Modern Art, 1951.

Diehl, Gaston, *Henri Matisse*. Universe Books, Inc., 1958.

Duthuit, Georges, and Pierre Reverdy, *The Last Works of Matisse*. Verve, Paris, 1958.

Escholier, Raymond, *Matisse: A Portrait of the Artist and the Man*. Translated by Geraldine and H. M. Colvile. Frederick A. Praeger, Publishers, 1960.

*Guichard-Meili, Jean, *Matisse*. Frederick A. Praeger, Publishers, 1967.

Lassaigne, Jacques, *Matisse*. Translated by Stuart Gilbert. Éditions d'Art Albert Skira, Geneva, 1959.

Lieberman, William S., *Matisse: 50 Years of his Graphic Art*. George Braziller, Inc., 1956.

Marchiori, Giuseppe, *Matisse*. Reynal & Company in association with William Morrow & Co., Inc. Amilcare Pizzi, Italy.

Wheeler, Monroe, *The Last Works of Henri Matisse—Large Cut Gouaches*. The Museum of Modern Art in collaboration with the Art Institute of Chicago and the San Francisco Museum of Art, 1961.

ART-HISTORICAL BACKGROUND

Crespelle, Jean-Paul, *The Fauves*. New York Graphic Society, 1962.

Duthuit, Georges. *The Fauvist Painters*. The Documents of Modern Art. Wittenborn, Schultz, Inc., 1950.

Haftman, Werner, Alfred Hentzen and William S. Lieberman, *German Art of the Twentieth Century*. Edited by Andrew C. Ritchie. The Museum of Modern Art, 1957.

Hamilton, George Heard, *Painting and Sculpture in Europe: 1880-1940*. The Pelican History of Art Series. Penguin Books, Inc., 1967.

Homer, William I., *Seurat and the Science of Painting*. M.I.T. Press, 1964.

*Muller, Joseph-Émile, *Fauvism*. Frederick A. Praeger, Publishers, 1967.

Rewald, John, *Post-Impressionism From Van Gogh to Gauguin* (second edition). The Museum of Modern Art, 1962.

*Russell, John, *Seurat*. Frederick A. Praeger, Publishers, 1965.

Selz, Peter, *German Expressionist Painting*. The University of California Press, 1957.

CULTURAL AND HISTORICAL BACKGROUND

Brinnin, John Malcolm, *The Third Rose*. Little, Brown and Co., 1959.

Pollack, Barbara, *The Collectors*. Bobbs-Merrill Company, Inc., 1962.

Saarinen, Aline B., *The Proud Possessors*. Random House, Inc., 1958.

Schack, William, *Art and Argyrol*. Sagamore Press, 1960.

*Stein, Gertrude, *The Autobiography of Alice B. Toklas*. Vintage Books.

EXHIBITION CATALOGUES

The Cone Collection (revised edition). The Baltimore Museum of Art, 1967.

Fauves and Expressionists. Leonard Hutton Galleries, April 18-June 12, 1968.

Henri Matisse. Texts by Jean Leymarie, Herbert Read, Williams S. Lieberman. Published with the cooperation of the UCLA Art Council, University of California Press, 1966.

Henri Matisse, 64 Paintings. Text by Lawrence Gowing. The Museum of Modern Art, 1966.

Matisse: 1869-1954. A retrospective exhibition at the Hayward Gallery. The Arts Council of Great Britain, 1968.

Neo-Impressionism. Text by Robert L. Herbert. The Solomon R. Guggenheim Museum, 1968.

Years of Ferment: The Birth of Twentieth Century Art, 1886-1914. An exhibition sponsored by the UCLA Art Council in collaboration with the UCLA Art Galleries. The UCLA Art Council, 1965.

Picture Credits

Acknowledgments

For their help in the production of this book the author and editors particularly wish to thank Mr. and Mrs. Pierre Matisse, New York, and Mr. and Mrs. Georges Duthuit, Paris. They also wish to thank Colette Audibert, Curator, Musée Matisse of Nice-Cimiez; Mr. and Mrs. Alfred H. Barr Jr., New York; Quentin Bell, University of Sussex; Mrs. Sidney F. Brody, Exhibitions Chairman, UCLA Art Council; Adeline Cacan, Conservateur, Musée du Petit Palais, Paris; Alice Derain, Chambourcy; Joan Diamant and Bruni Mayor, Pierre Matisse Gallery, New York; Director, Arts Council, Hayward Gallery, London; John W. Dodds, Stanford; Denise Fédit, Chargée de Mission, Musée National d'Art Moderne, Paris; Monroe W. Gill, New York; Lawrence Gowing, London; Mrs. Walter A. Haas, San Francisco; Mrs. St. John Hutchinson, London; Antonina Iserguina, The Hermitage Museum, Leningrad; Samuel Josefowitz, Lausanne; Mr. and Mrs. Xavier Lasbordes; Mrs. Albert D. Lasker, New York; Fulvio Nembrini, Arti Grafiche Amilcare Pizzi, Milan; Perry T. Rathbone, Director, Museum of Fine Arts, Boston; Ginette Signac, Paris; Staff of the Print Room, the Library, and the Rights and Reproductions Department, Museum of Modern Art, New York; Berthe Vlaminck; the owners of the original cut paper works shown on pages 173, 176, 177, 178-180 respectively; The Royal Museum of Fine Arts, Copenhagen; Museum of Modern Art, New York; Dallas Museum of Fine Arts and the Stedelijk Museum, Amsterdam.

Index

Numerals in italics indicate a picture of the subject mentioned. Unless otherwise identified, all listed art works are by Matisse. Dimensions are given in inches unless otherwise noted; height precedes width.

The text for this book was photocomposed in Bodoni Book, a typeface named for its Italian designer, Giambattista Bodoni (1740-1813). One of the earliest modern typefaces, Bodoni Book differs from more evenly weighted old-style characters in the greater contrast between thick and thin parts of letters. The Bodoni character is vertical with a thin, straight serif.

✗

PRODUCTION STAFF FOR TIME INCORPORATED

*John L. Hallenbeck (Vice President and Director of Production),
Robert E. Foy and Caroline Ferri
Text photocomposed under the direction of Albert J. Dunn*